The White Stripes

Sweethearts of the blues

Denise
Denise SULLIVAN

The White Stripes

Sweethearts of the blues

A BACKBEAT BOOK

First edition 2004

Published by Backbeat Books

600 Harrison Street,

San Francisco, CA94107, US

www.backbeatbooks.com

An imprint of The Music Player Network United

Entertainment Media Inc.

Published for Backbeat Books by Outline Press Ltd,

Unit 2a Union Court, 20-22 Union Road, London, SW4 6JP, England.

www.backbeatuk.com

ISBN 0-87930-805-2

ART DIRECTOR: Nigel Osborne

EDITOR: Paul Quinn

DESIGN: Paul Cooper Design

EDITORIAL DIRECTOR: Tony Bacon

Origination and Print by Colorprint (Hong Kong)

04 05 06 07 08 5 4 3 2 1

Contents

Prologue   **The Motor City is burning**   **4**
The rise and fall of Detroit

Chapter 1   **Broken bricks**   **12**
Mexicantown... upholstery... boy meets girl

    Picture gallery   **33**

Chapter 2   **Sympathetic sounds**   **50**
Influences... Dylan... Iggy... garage... bluesrock

Chapter 3   **Style and substance**   **68**
De Stijl art... Beck blues... colours, numbers, alchemy

Chapter 4   **Gonna need a bigger room**   **98**
White Blood Cells... from the deep South to the UK

Chapter 5   **Going to Wichita**   **124**
Elephant country... death of the sweetheart

Chapter 6   **21st century blues**   **146**
On tour... boll weevils... broken bones

Epilogue   **Home Sweet Home**   **160**

    Concordance   **162**
    Discography   **170**
    Index   **172**
    Acknowledgements   **175**

The Motor City
is burning

"There has to be that interval of neglect, there has to be discontinuity; it is religiously and artistically essential ... Ruins provide the incentive for restoration and for a return to origins."

J.B. JACKSON, FROM *THE NECESSITY FOR RUINS*, 1980

above: The MC5 (1964-1972)
right: one of Detroit's many ruins, the UniRoyal Tire Plant, 1980s

I t's not always the case that a rock band is inextricably linked to the place it calls home. But with The White Stripes and Detroit, the connection is fundamental.

Detroit was once one of those big and beautiful cities whose success, spirit and architecture were symbols of pride and progress for Americans. After suffering decades of neglect, that's all gone now, and the promise that it will come back looks pretty dim.

How bad can it really be, you might wonder. After all, many big cities have problems with drugs and crime, unemployment and poverty. Yet somehow Detroit seems more extreme. Imagine it was your city. Imagine it's gotten to the stage where most of your town's once-grand buildings have fallen into disrepair, been boarded up, covered in graffiti or burned-out, and the city's monuments defaced or torn down; on the streets there's the constant threat of violence, and you're afraid to go out at night – and even in the daytime. Some people try to rally to fix things up, while other people just say, yeah, right, tear down those eyesores – but then nothing ever happens… They don't fix them and they don't tear them down. It's like everything is on hold for 30-odd years. The same old situation every day.

But then what if these two alluring and graceful people who play intensified rock'n'roll suddenly emerge from the wreckage – and they say, yep, we come from this town, we know everyone thinks it's beyond hope, but it's our home…

Long before it became a skyscraper ghost-town, the murder capital of the world, and home to the current blues and garage rock explosion, Detroit was a mighty city and glorious riverfront emblem of the Industrial Revolution. It's a stage where America has played out its biggest dreams and greatest nightmares. Having burnt to the ground in 1805, Detroit adopted a motto: "We hope for better things; it will arise from its ashes."

Prior to its settlement by the French in 1701, Native Americans inhabited the land of what would become southeast Michigan. The area was a favorite destination on the fur-trading route because of its long coastline and easy access to waterways – the Detroit and St Clair Rivers, Michigan's lakes – and its accessibility to Canada. The French, led by Antoine de la Mothe Cadillac (a surname which would loom large in Detroit history), set up Fort Ponchartrain as one of its forts along the Canadian border to discourage British expansion from that direction. They ruled Ville D'Etroit, or Le Detroit (the straits), until it was captured by the British in 1760, along with Montreal, Quebec and Niagara. US rule began in 1796.

Incorporated as a city in 1815, Detroit was by that time known as the last stop on the underground railroad, the network established to lead African-American slaves north toward Canada and freedom. The music of western Africa, via the Deep South, was already beginning to make its presence felt in the North thanks to these travelers; with its roots planted there, the region's jazz and blues began to take shape and grow.

By the end of the 19th century, following the American Civil War, thousands of African-Americans migrated from the rural South seeking employment in the rapidly industrializing Northeast. Stoves were manufactured in Detroit, cigars were made, beer was brewed and the ports were bustling. With the city's plentiful factory jobs, immigrants arrived daily from Ireland, Germany, Poland, Ukraine, Greece and Armenia in particular; they brought their Catholic beliefs with them and called Detroit home.

In 1896, Henry Ford built his first car in Detroit, and with his invention of the assembly line and the opening of the Ford factory in 1903, the area was established as a home to the auto industry as well. General Motors and Chrysler opened shop alongside Dodge, Buick, Cadillac and more. Through the years, and through mergers and acquisitions, GM, Ford and Chrysler have absorbed the other US makers and become The Big Three. At one time GM bore the distinction, "largest corporation in the world."

With the assembly line came some other made-in-Detroit auto-centric innovations, like the first traffic light, the first stretch of concrete paved road, and the first urban freeway. And with the automobile came the labor movement: an historic sit-in at GM headquarters in Flint, Michigan led to the establishment of the United Auto Workers (UAW) in the late 1930s.

Grand structures styled in gothic and Venetian architecture lined the city's streets – the Book Cadillac Hotel, the Statler Hotel, the Kales, the Metropolitan and the Wurlitzer Buildings: symbols of the area's prosperity, and one of the best collections of pre-WWII architecture in the US. A hard-working town, Detroit was also a hard-playing, good-time town known for its music, mayhem and dancing in the streets. During the jazz age and the swing era Detroit hopped to the beat at its unusually high concentration of grand ballrooms and dancehalls with evocative names like The Bob-Lo Pavilion, the Arcadia, the Pier Ballroom, The Graystone and the Grande (pronounced Grandee) Ballroom – later at the center of the Sixties rock scene – drawing headliners like Duke Ellington, Cab Calloway and Glenn Miller. Movie palaces like the Fox and the Majestic also played host to the vaudeville acts of the day (many of these buildings survive surprisingly intact today, having been spared the wrecking ball – presumably because they provided a rare source of affordable entertainment).

The 1940s also gave rise to the Hastings Street scene in Paradise Valley. In the time of racial segregation, the area was the home to all black-owned businesses and Detroit blues; the all-night jam sessions would play on, sometimes well into the next day. Detroit pianist Charlie Spand accompanied Blind Blake on his swingin' boogie woogie, 'Hastings Street,' with lines like: "*Make me feel like I wanna go back to Dee-troit.*"

John Lee Hooker, a recent transplant from Clarksdale, Mississippi, made a name for himself with his 1948 side 'Boogie Chillen,' another tribute to Detroit nightlife. Hooker's primitive, big-beat boogie would become a hallmark of Detroit Rock, though he remains one of its most underrated influences. Just one man, he sounded more like a band on his primitive, one-chord hypno-drones. His music reverberates throughout the history of the region's rock.

Hooker also shared a kinship with Britain's early blues rockers, The Yardbirds and The Animals. In fact, yet another reason Detroit is such a fertile ground for rock is that they have long had a direct link to the UK – even well before globalization. Due to the city's proximity to Windsor, Ontario, Detroiters had full access to Canadian broadcast services and its British connection.

Berry Gordy's Motown of the 1960s is the city's most visible cultural export. Smokey Robinson, Diana Ross and Stevie Wonder are but three of the Michigan natives who were stars on the Tamla/Motown roster. The label's house writers, Holland-Dozier-Holland, and house band, the Funk Brothers, were just some of the musicians at Gordy's fingertips who helped create a sound that would be identifiable the world over. But not all fared so well. Some of the world-class musicians who helped shape the sound of rockin' soul all over the world reportedly died penniless or living on the streets. Motown itself would roll out of Detroit and head for Los Angeles in 1971.

The good times had officially come to an end. Although the population had continued to increase, eventually topping out at 1.5 million people, the city had been in a steady economic decline since World War II and was left ill-equipped to house and employ its people. Between 1948 and 1967, over a million jobs in manufacturing were lost. The massive-scaled inner-city Packard plant stopped making cars in 1956 and as automation took over, more jobs evaporated. The auto industry, with foreign makers consistently threatening to edge into the Big Three's market, had also begun its steady downturn, which showed little sign of improving. Jobs would continue to be lost throughout Michigan in the ensuing decades.

Race riots had erupted in town as far back as 1863; a 1943 riot left casualties and steadily rising ill-will between whites and blacks. In a city that was already essentially segregated, attacks on blacks became more frequent and fierce in the early to mid 1960s. A disproportionate number of white police were said to have harassed and exerted an unnecessary force on the growing majority African-American population. With the city's younger African-American entry-level factory workers now jobless and on the streets, frustrations mounted, crime escalated and the gap between rich and poor, black and white deepened. The Detroit Riots of 1967 were the result of years of racial tension and economic inequality, and the toll they took on this once fair city was its death knell, signaling the new era of unprecedented decline.

Sparked by a raid on an after-hours bar in the Twelfth Street area, and culminating with the Algiers Motel incident at which three people were slain, the riots lasted nearly one week, and by the end there were 43 African-Americans dead, 700 arrested and over 1000 injured. This was the second major race riot in Detroit in 25 years to require additional law enforcement, including the National Guard, to restore the peace.

In this once model city, things fell apart rapidly. President Lyndon Johnson's

Great Society, with its plans to improve the problems of health and education, and its War on Poverty, failed Detroit – despite having established government programs to aid the poor with job training, housing, education and healthcare. Businesses big and small pulled out en masse; the term 'white flight' was adopted to describe the massive migration to the suburbs of Detroit. The city's population dropped dramatically (it is currently under a million). As these inner city events unfolded, US involvement in the Vietnam War escalated, and collective despair was at an all-time high. Civil rights leaders and community activists were paralyzed with grief, while the angry and oppressed African-American community and empathic youth culture turned toward radicalism and rock'n'roll.

The anti-war sentiment shared by the nation's young people and the dire straits of inner-city Detroit living created an atmosphere that was ripe for radicalization. Like its sister organizations in Oakland and Berkeley California – home to the Black Panthers and Free Speech Movement respectively – militant activist groups like the Panthers and the sympathetic Weathermen used Detroit as an important base for operations (coincidentally Oakland and Berkeley are also names of Detroit suburbs). By reaching out to the disenfranchised and calling attention to the system that had failed them, they employed a by-any-means-necessary strategy to achieve their goals toward reform. The rebel stance meant their collective efforts would eventually all be brought to a halt by the FBI, and their movements forced underground.

Among the activists was poet John Sinclair; his Trans-Love Energies collective managed the MC5 and left Detroit (along with everyone else) for nearby Ann Arbor to form the White Panther Party – whose credo advocated sex, drugs and rock'n'roll. Sinclair and the MC5 parted ways as he continued to become politicized (John Lennon and Yoko Ono would come to his aid at the legendary *Free John Sinclair Rally* in Ann Arbor in 1971) . But alongside their little brothers in Iggy & The Stooges, The MC5 would make a lasting impression on the supercharged and high-strung rock'n'roll that was getting to be known as the Detroit Rock Sound.

Even the R&B was off-the-wall, when George Clinton's Parliament/Funkadelic added some noise to the freak scene. Iggy and The MC5's individual stories and influence will be referred to in more depth throughout this story, as they are among the guiding captains of the Detroit rocket ship. Both bands enjoyed a solid three-album run but by 1973 they had both called it a night. And so did everybody else in Detroit Rock City, for what it was now worth.

Though Detroit would become the beneficiary of more government anti-poverty and redevelopment funds than any other city besides New York, the decline had been in effect for too long for the city to recover. In the days, months and years following the riots, the after-effects were still being felt. Lives and loved ones were lost and American dreams shattered. Small business owners could not afford to rebuild and were forced to abandon the inner city; big businesses opted to relocate as the big recession of the 1970s got underway. Its reputation as a high-crime city became embedded in the culture, its pervasiveness bordering on urban mythology but in part based on the nationally-published FBI annual report on crime – and Detroit's consistent ranking as the Murder Capital of the USA.

The sound of the city was in the process of being defamed by arena rockers like Bob Seger and Motor City Madman Ted Nugent. Homegrown *Creem* magazine, with its new style of irreverent, myth-busting music journalism, did cement Detroit's reputation as Rock City – although when its leading light Lester Bangs quit in 1976 he took the magazine's soul with him.

But the rhythm of the city can't be killed – after all, those primal beats were there from the very beginning. To be from Michigan is to be a maverick. As the birthplace of so much invention, there is magic in the air there (or at least in all those waterways). Someday Detroit's nightmare would be transformed into a dream again – but this business of rebuilding, of recovering, of returning to origins would belong to the next generation.

The city where rioters once appropriated a DJ's catchphrase, "Burn Baby Burn" – and where every October 30th, Devil's Night, arsonists set fires all over town – would rise from the ashes, as its motto claimed. There might be a sleeping period, a lull, but the rhythm would return to Detroit once more.

And so the city's embattled but resilient people rocked on into the 21st century, when two of its young residents, John Gillis and Meg White, were about to restore some much needed pride…

Chapter 1

Broken
bricks

"There was a little girl and there
was a little boy and they lived in an
alley under the red sky."

BOB DYLAN, 'UNDER THE RED SKY'

above: Iggy Pop, in his early Stooges days
right: downtown Detroit, viewed from the southwest,
looking over Old Tiger Stadium

**J**ust west of downtown, past Old Tiger Stadium to the right, the Detroit River on the left, the street numbers start to go up; into the teens, into the twenties, on down the Vernor Highway, and you end up in Mexicantown – a multi-cultural mecca, and as lively a neighborhood as you're likely to see five minutes from Detroit's bleak city center. Mexican restaurants serve noontime and late-night meals, kids practice baseball on the field at Clark Park, while prostitutes and crackheads loiter on the curb outside the Hotel Yorba.

This is Jack White's neighborhood. Born John Gillis on July 9th 1975, he was the tenth and youngest child of Teresa and Gordon McKenzie Gillis of Southwest Detroit. The family lived in a modest home on Ferdinand Street, just a couple of blocks from the aforementioned Clark Park, where Jack used to play as a kid. Some call it the worst neighborhood in Detroit, but for those who call it home, Mexicantown is its own special corner of the city.

"The neighborhood was all Mexican," says Jack. "The school was Mexican and black and they were all into rap and house music, which I couldn't stand. I had such a stiff upper lip about it for 18 years. I don't know why I didn't just break down and have some friends but I just couldn't do it … I didn't really have much of a great time in grade school. Kids are just so cruel sometimes. It's nice to fantasize that they're not."

Lording over the neighborhood is Holy Redeemer, an early-20th-century-model, grand Catholic church. Established in the 1880s and dedicated in 1923, the parish served a mostly Irish and German community back then. Today, it is one of those rare, fantastically preserved vestiges of Detroit's early 20th century grandeur. Its massive cathedral, school buildings, convent and rectory are all constructed out of red brick and kept in immaculate condition. Former neighbors will tell you the Gillis family attended mass every Sunday, even in the freewheeling 1970s. Jack remembers it a little differently.

"There was this place by my house called Dooley's Coney Island [a Coney Island is another name for the regional delicacy – a hot dog], and when I was supposed to be going to church, I used to go to Dooley's."

The old neighborhood is also home to the Hotel Yorba, on Lafayette Street.

It's easy to imagine how, as a child, Jack may have been curious about what went on inside the former riverfront hospitality house turned cheap flophouse.

"The Hotel Yorba is a really disgusting hotel. There was a great rumor when I was a kid that The Beatles had stayed there. They never did, but I loved that rumor." There's another story that circulates in the neighborhood: that Elvis visited the Fisher auto assembly plant there to watch his custom Cadillac roll off the line. Neither story can be confirmed, but the idea that *both* the Beatles and Elvis *could* have roamed Southwest Detroit is perfect: if you don't like one reality, just make up another one – it just might fit.

These days, the only people you'll see at the Hotel Yorba are transients. And the only people on the nearby streets are those who need to be there, like residents and workmen. But even if you're a homeboy, there's still a chance of getting caught in some crossfire, as Jack points out.

I didn't really have much of a great time in grade school. Kids are just so cruel sometimes

"There's these punk kids who break windows and stuff like that – you know, [they] make fun of me when I walk into the gas station. It's like, I've lived here my whole life, and he's eight years old and talking to me like that. They'll bust your window, and then you go take them to their parents and their parents take their side. They get away with murder." One day Jack would write the song 'I Think I Smell A Rat' about little kids like that.

Things were different when he was growing up in Mexicantown: his mother and father, a secretary and a maintenance man respectively, raised their ten children – seven boys and three girls – to love thy neighbor and to honor a code of general good behavior. That's not to say there wasn't some good rock'n'roll going down in the Gillis household: the six older boys were in a band called Catalyst, and the sisters were said to be regulars at clubs and bars in East Dearborn which consistently served up blues on the bill of fare. Albert Collins, Leon Russell and Dr John all frequently rolled through town, while high-charged house bands filled the bars on the other nights. Flip on the car radio on the way home and you might tune into a homegrown program, like the *Famous Coachman*, who spun blues sides late into the night on WDET. The blues was in the air in late 1970s/early 1980s Detroit, and its allure was not lost on the littlest Gillis.

Jack taught himself to play the drums when he was five. He wasn't completely single-minded about music, though. He loved the games that little boys do: war, toy soldiers and building forts in the backyard. His friend from the fifth grade, Dominic Suchyta, remembers Jack as a classical music fan, "of all things... I thought that was really strange," he says.

Dominic and Jack went to Holy Redeemer school together and hung out all the time. Their houses were just a bike ride away from each other; they were boy scouts together, they played hockey, they listened to music together and they taped it off TV – the usual boy stuff.

We listened to Stevie Ray Vaughan, but that ended quick. It was just too processed for us

"I rode my bike to his house every day," says Suchyta. "I shared a room with two other brothers and was trying to get away from my house, and so I spent a lot of time at the Gillis's. His brothers and sisters were children of the Seventies and they were into white boy blues, like the British Invasion stuff, which we weren't that into. We got into classic rock early on – Led Zeppelin – and I'm glad we did: got that out of the way. We listened to Stevie Ray Vaughan, but that ended quick. It was just too processed for us.

"Only one or two of his siblings was living at home. The attic had been occupied by some of his older brothers, but it was empty except for all sorts of guitars and drums and recording equipment."

Soon the pair started riding their bikes to nearby Dearborn to buy musical equipment, returning home "loaded up with hi-hats and stuff." They started recording in seventh grade (around the age of 12 or 13), when Jack was still a shorthaired kid with braces.

"I remember cleaning up the attic so we could start recording," says Suchyta.

"Jack was playing guitar and drums and I was playing guitar and bass. We recorded all sorts of stuff."

The blues captured their imagination from the start. "Jack's brother Ed told us to buy a Howlin' Wolf tape because we were playing 'Sittin' On Top Of The World' and all we were going on was the Cream album," recalls Suchyta.

The boys also felt a connection to John Lee Hooker, because they knew he was from Detroit, but they didn't listen to him much. " I remember buying a Chess box set," says Suchyta. "We got way into Chicago blues and country blues – we were so into blues."

By 1990 they had begun recording Bob Dylan songs on the four-track. "We recorded 'Masters Of War' in ninth grade... I think we were about 15. We did 'Groom Still Waiting At The Altar' and 'From A Buick Six.' Jack had that Dylan album *Under The Red Sky.*"

Soon they'd graduate to songs by righteous punks Fugazi and The Beastie Boys' 'Groove Holmes.' A teenaged Dylan fan with a blossoming interest in deep blues, Jack was now a student at Cass Tech. This Detroit public high drew students from around the Detroit area, and counts among its graduates musicians such as Donald Byrd and Ron Carter, actors Ellen Burstyn and Lily Tomlin, and Detroit mayor Kwame Kilpatrick. Jack and Dominic did have each other, but Jack found it increasingly hard to relate to his hip-hop-loving peers. In the early 1980s techno music exploded out of the Detroit clubs, and by the 1990s it was the soundtrack to the rave culture that thrived in Detroit's burned-out warehouses and abandoned buildings. That wasn't for Jack either.

"We were kinda outcasts at high school," says Suchyta. "Our experience there was really weird." Not entirely negative, though – the boys used the old city as their personal "abandoned amusement park," exploring its streets before heading home to Southwest.

Suchyta has some fond memories of the time. "There was a blues guitar player, he was blind, who used to sit out in front of a toy store on Woodward Avenue, near where we had to go to catch the bus back," he says. "Two intelligent white kids in Detroit have it easier than you'd think. I mean, there were threats but... we knew who to stay away from. And we kept ourselves busy with recordings.

A lot of people say they are from Detroit, but we were really Detroit kids...

"We went to pawn shops, and an old bookstore downtown, John King Books. There were used records on the third floor – we'd always go there and get records for a buck." He believes that explains Jack's attraction to the old stuff, the knock-offs, "like those off-brand guitars, the weird second-hand stuff." Among Jack's most prized pieces of equipment are his beloved Ward's Airline guitar and Silvertone amp – both defunct Sixties models from US department stores.

Upholstery, Resin & Peas

Always looking for an escape hatch, Jack stayed in school but grabbed at the chance when one of his brother's friends, Brian Muldoon, offered him a job as an upholsterer's apprentice. Working alongside Muldoon, 16 years his senior, White not only got an education in upholstering, he learned about areas of music that he and Dominic had yet to explore.

"Brian had all these great records and turned us on to all this stuff – the dirt and the sleaze," explains Suchyta. "He got us into the Flat Duo Jets, The MC5 and The Gories."

Jack was taken with all of them. The Flat Duo Jets, from North Carolina, were a psychobilly guitar-and-drum duo all hepped-up on Link Wray and Elvis, but with a twist of twang. The MC5 is of course the stuff of Detroit rock legend, notable for its grinding take on old-time rock and Rob Tyner's intensified vocal style. And The Gories are a legendarily primitive, bass-less Detroit band – a three-piece co-formed by Mick Collins in 1986. Muldoon also played them records by the mighty Stooges and the early 1980s LA band The Gun Club, both groups known for marrying a big primitive rock beat with the blues.

Soon, Suchyta, White and Muldoon started to play music together; 'Looking At You' by the MC5 was one of their covers. When Suchyta left for college, the pair carried on as a two-piece, with no bass, dubbing themselves Two Part Resin.

"They rehearsed without me and then if I came back I would play," says Suchyta. "We were listening to so much bass-less music, it wasn't really a big deal."

Around the same time, Jack had also gotten to be a good enough drummer to join local band Goober & The Peas, a fledgling country punk act with two independent albums. The band had just about run out of road, but not before Jack, or 'Doc' as he was known in the Peas, could tour with them as a drummer.

Goober leader Dan Miller says Jack had the right instincts for his group – "not too technical." And because he got along well with the rest of the band personnel, it was a no-brainer when it came to him joining.

"I think it was a good thing for him just to see what it was like to be in a band that toured, and probably see what kind of mistakes we made. I do remember the first show when he played drums. For an encore he came up and sang some Elvis song. People where just shocked by his passion for it," recalls Miller.

"It was weird, knowing him at 19 and seeing this person who had all these really clear-cut goals and this real commitment and passion for how he wanted things to go in his life, musically and otherwise. I remember him saying, 'I really want to be proud of everything I do.'"

Jack tells a story of how once when on tour with Goober & The Peas in California he found a much-needed 100-spot on the street, and he immediately spent it on a copy of Iggy Pop's 1982 autobiography, *I Need More*.

"I was just freaking out. I was so inspired. I was doing somersaults on the front lawn," remembers Jack. "And these guys I was with were like, "Look how happy Jack is, he found a bunch of money.' They didn't know what I was so excited about, y'know, what I'd just read."

In a few seasons, Jack had gone from learning about the music from his hometown in the confines of Muldoon's studio to becoming a player on the scene there. For Jack on his visionquest, the days and nights

People had the same attitude they had at high school. Small-minded stuff. Nobody was serious about what they wanted

must have felt interminable, but things were heating up fast – just not fast enough for him to quit his day job. He had tried college for one semester, but in his estimation, "People had the same attitude they had at high school. Small-minded

19

stuff. Nobody was serious about what they wanted." So for now, he would stick with upholstery. At the age of 21, Jack started his own business, Third Man Upholstery.

"I didn't understand why he wasn't going to go to college or why he wanted to become an upholsterer," says Suchyta. "I remember he had a sign above his bed on the ceiling that said, 'Learn To Love Upholstery.' At the time I thought, what a weirdo… but I get it now. I didn't understand a lot of things he did until much later. He was very intentional, very deliberate. We wouldn't just listen to music, we would study it."

In a long interview on the subject of upholstering in *The Believer* magazine in 2003, Jack told author and publisher Dave Eggers, "When I'd re-upholster furniture, I'd take off the old fabric and … write poems and things inside the furniture, so if it was ever re-upholstered again one day they'd get little messages from the last person who upholstered it." His favorite repairs were the mid-century modern items, things by the likes of Noel and Herman Miller – "the most difficult upholstery you can do," according to Jack.

I never really loved the money part … I guess it started to hurt my business attitude

Even then, his business approach was unconventional: "I started trying to make an art form out of giving someone a bill for my services, like writing it with crayon on a piece of paper, or having a yellow piece of paper with black marker saying, 'You owe me $300.' People would be like, 'What the hell is this?' People just didn't dig it. It was two different worlds colliding. I got so much into the cartooniness of the business, almost to the point of it being a joke to the people who would see me, and they wouldn't really trust me to do a good job.

"I never really loved the money part," he says, by way of explaining his ultimate decision to abandon the enterprise. "I guess it started to hurt my business attitude."

Without the upholstery career to worry about, Jack shifted his energies hot and heavy towards an education in the leaner and meaner sounds of the Detroit garage rock revival. A real primitive rock element had infiltrated the Detroit club scene in the late 1980s and early 1990s, following a fallow period of new wave and punk that didn't really ever break out (save for the power pop of the red-leathered Romantics). The new groups, like the Flaming Groovies-fueled Rocket 455, the blues-laced two-piece Bantam Rooster, the clean-cut Hentchmen, the outrageous "Catholic sibling runaways" Demolition Doll Rods, and the ultra-trash Gories were playing kick-out-the-jams rock'n'roll, most all of them without a bass player (only Rocket 455 had a bassist). With Suchyta away at school, Muldoon and White kept at it. But it was Jack who had formed a new alliance – and she was about to help him open doors and move his vision toward completely new worlds.

Got a little feeling goin'

Megan White was born on December 10th 1974, seven months earlier than Jack. On the surface it seems that their worlds couldn't have been more different: she was raised in Grosse Point, a well-off, laidback, rural suburb way over on the other side of Detroit City with her parents, Walter Hackett White Jr and Catherine Della, both from Michigan, and her sole sibling, Heather.

Meg says her favorite childhood game was a reconstruction of the Fortress Of Solitude from *Superman*. "I would shovel up all the winter snow into a big mountain and then tunnel all the way through," she recalls. "I was obsessed with it. It was the best."

Her school days were fairly under-whelming, according to her own account. She was a good girl, "super shy," liked to shop for records and go to the movies. When she went to college and to catering school,

Meg was raised in Grosse Point, a well-off, laidback, rural suburb on the other side of Detroit

she thought she might become a chef. She ended up a bartender – "the shyest bartender on the planet," by her own admission – and that's how she met Jack.

Very little is known about the couple's initial meeting or courtship but it's easy to imagine: all you have to do is watch them play together and if you squint very hard, you might just see the cord that connects them. Squint harder and there's Jack on a barstool, one arm on the bar, the other foot and eye toward the empty dancefloor and the door as the last customers straggle, grabbing coats on their ways out the door. Meg's behind the bar, head tilted just so, polishing glasses till the lights go on, her shift officially over.

Described as quiet by those who know her, and also as someone who enjoys a good time – a drink, a smoke – it's said Meg is a woman of few words. But when she speaks, like in that old television ad, people listen. Of course Jack hears something from Meg that only he can hear. As Iggy Pop himself said to him, "It's not like you just got *some* drummer, you know what I'm saying? It's a whole particular thing. You know what I'm saying?!" Uh-huh.

Meg says she wasn't influenced by female musicians in particular, though if she had to pick one it would be, "maybe Mo Tucker, I don't know." She loves all kinds of music, has a particular fondness for country's long-tressed songbirds Loretta Lynn and Emmylou Harris, but the fact is she never planned on getting into music at all, it just ended up that way when she picked up the drumsticks in 1996. She was 21 and it was the year she and Jack married – at which point Jack took her

I'd kind of like it if people saw us and just halfway through the set started laughing

surname and became Mr White. The pair were living in the Gillis family home on Ferdinand Street at the time: when the Gillis parents retired, they arranged it so Jack, their youngest, could buy the house and live in it with his bride.

"They left a piano and I started to play," says Jack, matter-of-factly. "That was really the whole idea when we started the band, it was just some way of getting back to childhood without it being a comedy act. It was about how kids look at things. There's a sense of humor that is deeply buried under everything. I'd kind of like it if people saw us and just halfway through the set started laughing."

Perhaps it was this 'childish' ideal that prompted Jack and Meg to present themselves as brother and sister rather than the couple they were. Jack says he's surprised more journalists don't inquire about the pair's childhoods. Perhaps they prefer to play along…

"Jack had a set of drums upstairs," Meg goes on, "so I began playing with him."

"We were just messing around, kind of as a joke," says Jack, "but it ended up being perfect. She played like such a child – it was something fresh."

"It was childlike because I had no idea what I was doing…" says Meg. "I had *no* idea it would get this big. Come on – we're a two-piece blues band from Detroit."

But it's the directness of the duo format, and Meg's role within it, that has helped create the unique appeal of

It's almost as if Jack needed to be put in a box – that box he puts himself in

The White Stripes. "People don't give Meg enough credit," says Dominic Suchyta. "She has a big hand in their sound, in the simplification of all the songs. I don't think Jack would be doing the kind of writing he's doing without Meg's input. I saw what he was doing before he met her and it was great and everything, but it just didn't have that spark they have. It's almost as if he needed to be put in a box, that box he puts himself in."

The box analogy is one The White Stripes return to again and again. "From day one, we purposely got involved in this box and with these limitations and chose not to grow and evolve," says Jack. (Lux Interior and Poison Ivy of The Cramps issued a similar edict when they started their rockin' bones combo in 1976 – and nearly 30 years later they're still the same.)

The music Jack and Meg would make together would be simple, stripped-down and direct: punk, blues and garage rock is what they liked anyway. Its three primary elements – rhythm, melody and storytelling – were inspired by the blues.

The story goes that on the very first day the pair sat down to play together, a tiny jam evolved into 'Screwdriver,' a song that never fails to hit home when the band perform it live. Jack explains it was based on a real life-threatening incident that happened on the mean streets of Mexicantown.

"We just started doing that riff and there was this screwdriver laying there, so

23

I started singing about it – what I'd do with it, ya know, being angry. When I was a kid I saw somebody – I think it was a comic strip or something – some kids on a subway and they were gonna rob somebody but they had screwdrivers in their hands, not knives."

The Gold Dollar

As legend has it The White Stripes first played together on Bastille Day, July 14th, 1997. But their first known public performance was on August 15th, opening for The Hentchmen at local garage-band central the Gold Dollar, situated at the heart of Detroit's run-down, crime-ridden Cass Corridor. Coming from Southwest, they had some idea of what they would be in for before they got there.

"You'd play the Gold Dollar, you'd walk out the door and your [car/truck] window would be smashed and all your stuff would be gone," says Jason Stollsteimer of The Von Bondies, the White Stripes' Detroit rock contemporaries. "Bands would be upset, crying sometimes, cause all their [stuff's] gone, and we'd kinda just walk by... 'What do you expect, look at where you parked...'"

Stollsteimer, who grew up in Ypsilanti – as did Iggy Pop – was a new arrival on the scene himself. A garage-rock hound, he'd make the hour drive on a Friday or Saturday night to see The Hentchmen or Bantam Rooster.

"For bands like that to get 100 people was amazing – and they did. Those were the only two bands we really knew. I heard of The Detroit Cobras, but the only thing I knew was that they were a covers band."

"For a long time we'd be the warm-up band," says Meg, "because people had the idea in their heads that a two-piece band could never be the headliners of anything.

Dave Buick, owner of the Italy Records label and proprietor of record shop Young Soul Rebels, was among the 20 or 30 people who were at the early shows. He says he liked The White Stripes because their primitive shake, rattle and roll reminded him of The Gories. He saw The White Stripes twice on the first weekend they performed live.

"Most people were outside," remembers Buick. "I was one of them – I watched the first couple of songs and then went outside. I think it took me a couple of times to warm up to them… I don't know what it was. After that I started going to all of their shows. There was nothing fancy and that was really cool. Jack had a really powerful presence even back then. The whole vision of the band, the visuals, the red and white, red pants, white shirt… Meg had the peppermint drums from the very first time.

"A lot of people didn't understand them and didn't like them, thought that Jack was just whining, didn't really get it, didn't understand [why there was] no bass player."

By October, Buick asked if he could put out a single for them. He'd just released two records on his Italy label and The White Stripes would be the third.

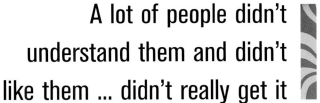

A lot of people didn't understand them and didn't like them … didn't really get it

"I asked Jack about it – he said he didn't have enough money, and walked away," says Buick. "And then I had to explain to him that I'd pay for it. He was really naïve about the whole process."

Now a member of three bands – The White Stripes plus the glam-rock The Go from Grand Rapids (with fellow singer-guitarist Bobby Harlow) and another go-around with his friend Dan Miller in the country-ish Two Star Tabernacle – Jack was traveling more and sowing his musical oats wherever he could.

On a trip to Toledo with Two Star, Jack met Johnny Walker and Ben Swank. Walker and Swank had first collaborated in a blues punk band, Henry & June, and were starting up their duo, The Soledad Brothers. "We were talking and told him we did a two-piece blues combo and he said he did too, so we just kinda started hanging out, and booking some shows together," says Swank.

"Where we come from, it's pretty easy to cross paths with people who have similar interests," says Walker of the 'Rust Belt' region – the collective name for the northern states whose heavy industry has collapsed. "We're all into the same rock. He was really into my slide playing and we swapped ideas. He had a four-track reel-to-reel in his living room … We'd go out and play on tracks – like kids do everywhere, every day."

Buick released the first White Stripes single, 'Let's Shake Hands' (b/w 'Look Me Over Closely,' a version of an old Marlene Dietrich number) in 1998, and followed it with 'Lafayette Blues,' a frantic rant about the French-named streets of Detroit. The b-side, 'Sugar Never Tasted So Good,' is an acoustic wind-up "about some crazy mumbo-jumbo of wrinkled brains and puppet strings," as Buick describes it on the Italy website.

The Soledads also came out with an Italy Records single in 1998 – 'Sugar And Spice' b/w 'Johnny's Death Letter' – then signed to garage-rock specialists Estrus the following year. Jack worked on producing tracks with them on-and-off for nearly two years; he even agreed to dress up as a demented Uncle Sam on the album's cover. Former MC5 management mastermind and blues enthusiast John Sinclair wrote the liner notes and The Soledads' self-titled release saw the light of day in 2000.

"We were just getting together, messing around, bouncing off ideas. Learning how to record and things like that," says Swank – who, in later years, as it happens, ended up living at the Ferdinand Street house formerly occupied by Jack and Meg.

Bolstered by a few good reviews for the singles in fanzines and an invitation by serious-minded indie band Pavement to support them on tour, Jack and Meg were ready to take their own show on the road and play their first dates outside Detroit.

"I don't know when I first realized they were going to keep on going the way they're going," says Buick. "It mighta been the first big tour they went on. They did a few East Coast dates with Pavement and they said that a bunch of people had driven eight or ten hours just to see The White Stripes."

After the release of the second single, Buick said he was getting mail, "from all over the place – all over the country and overseas – to find out how they could get 'em. After we did the first single, Jack produced pretty much every single I put out, and people really got into what he did that way too." Ironically, things were going a little slower at home: "It took about a year for anyone around here to get into them," says Buick. Most people couldn't even get their name right at first, billing them alternately as White Stripe, White Strike, White Strikes, Light Strikes and, worst yet, White Lines. Maybe they should've just stuck with The Peppermints, named after Meg's favorite sweet.

But The White Stripes always had friends and supporters among their fellow musicians. "I talked my bandmates into bringing them on tour," says Janet Weiss, drummer with Sleater-Kinney. She was among the ten or so people who saw the Stripes in an early performance at Al's Bar in Los Angeles. "Seeing them play in a tiny club, even to a small crowd, it was obvious they had a cool thing going on. Lots of charisma, and catchy songs, Jack's amazing guitar work, and I liked the way Meg would break up the drum parts with tom breaks," she says.

"Meg's drumming style is unabashedly her own. She takes heat for keeping it simple, but that's what creates the tension within the music. She's tugging at the beat while Jack's pushing it."

Despite her enthusiasm for the duo, Weiss explains that inviting a band they didn't know to tour with them had its risks. "We had never met them, and had no idea how they would be to hang out with. We were very skeptical about this brother and sister thing. They won us over quickly… turning out to be smart and sweet, and really fun. I enjoyed having a guy around backstage playing Dylan songs and being a little cocky."

I enjoyed having a guy around backstage playing Dylan songs and being a little cocky

The band found another supporter a little closer to home in Steve Shaw of The Detroit Cobras. The Cobras had been up-and-running since 1995: two women, three guys playing the bejeezus out of the Motor City's rare grooves and lost soul sides – all covers, all the time. In 1998 the group released an album, *Mink Rat Or Rabbit*, on the Long Beach, California indie label, Sympathy For The Record Industry, known for its stable of gutbucket, garagey primitive rock bands. Shaw introduced Long Gone John (the label's founder and sole employee) to The White Stripes.

As Jack himself tells it, "Steve told him, 'There's this two-piece band in Detroit, it's a boy and a girl, and they're brother and sister.' And John said, 'Who sings, and who plays drums?' Steve told him, and John goes, 'Aw, it would've been better if it was the other way round.' When he heard my voice, he said, 'Fine!'."

In iconoclastic fashion, Long Gone John went ahead and OK'd the recording of an album without ever having seen the band play live. The White Stripes ran down the songs for Jim Diamond, who engineered the sessions at his Ghetto Recorders in Detroit City. "It was pretty rough," says Diamond. "We were certainly going for a stinky kind of sound."

> It was pretty rough. We were certainly going for a stinky kind of sound

And so The White Stripes self-titled debut album was born, with minimal fuss. "The whole thing cost less than two grand to make. It's a fantastic record, and it's still probably my favorite," says Long Gone.

Whether Long Gone was more impressed by the record's financial economy or its straight-to-the-point, it-takes-two attitude, it's easy to grasp why he loved it so. It has the sound of confidence, rather than cockiness. Some bands never get it right their whole careers – but The White Stripes had a vision, and you could hear it from the get-go.

Consider the presentation – the red, the white, the black. The rhythm, the melody and the songwriting were all in place, and The White Stripes' three main song forms were all represented: the blues, the rockers and the minor-key ballads/old-time tunes. The cover songs – Dylan's 'One More Cup of Coffee,' Robert Johnson's 'Stop Breakin' Down,' and the standard, 'St James Infirmary Blues' – revealed some initial clues as to where they were coming from. The practice of including lyrics and a nice cryptic liner-note/story was delivered in its first installment here. No one knew it then but this complete package, and introduction to the world of rhythmical and melodious storytelling with attention to detail, was all by design.

"I'd been writing all these childish songs, like 'Jimmy The Exploder,' this story I made up about a monkey who exploded things that weren't the color red," says Jack. "So when Meg started playing that way, I was like, 'Man, don't even practice – this is perfect.' She was playing so childishly."

If the throbbing bass drum and Iggy-like whoops on 'Jimmy' don't grab you, then the next one will. The second track is a 12-bar blues, Robert Johnson's 'Stop

Breakin' Down.' Jack claims, "I had actually never heard the Rolling Stones' version of 'Stop...' until after our LP came out ... You know, I'd heard *Exile On Main Street* before, but didn't own it."

It's safe to say there are elements that draw from both the Stones and Johnson, but trying to figure out what's from where will drive you mad. This is simply a new kind of blues, White Stripes-style.

"The bluesmen have always been doing that," says Jack, "stripping songwriting down to those three components... storytelling, melody and rhythm. I hate the fact that the bluesman has been parodied – 'Oh I woke up this morning and my baby's gone,' *Blues Brothers* kind of thing – when those guys are the gods of music. I mean, there should be statues of them everywhere."

There's nothing new in borrowing from the blues; it's not like punk and indie-rockers hadn't tried it before. You can certainly look back to Jeffrey Lee Pierce's Gun Club, the two-piece, sun-soaked Arizona duo Doo Rag, even arty Jon Spencer, all of whom have attempted to hijack the blues for a new generation. But the secret to The White Stripes' blues wasn't in the mix, and it wasn't a mission. Singing the blues was their birthright. Being from Detroit, The White Stripes needed something to help them dream their way out of their environment, a service the blues had long provided for its practioneers, who've used it to sing their way up and out of bad situations for over 100 years.

The blues, with its rhythmic, storytelling tradition, evolved from songs that came to America with slaves abducted from West Africa. In those songs you could hear the

I hate the fact that the bluesman has been parodied, when those guys are the gods of music

sorrow of estrangement from homeland and family, and the treachery of enslavement. Music offered a way for the beleaguered and suffering to cope, as they hollered in unison or in call-and-response in the fields, or working on the chain gang. Those songs eventually gave birth to the blues, the secret language of the oppressed. The songs were infused with hidden meanings and a poetic spirit that protected the innocent and indicted the guilty. We can't ignore the fact that the construction of America's most extravagant cities, and the growth of its successful industries, was originally dependent on the labor of former slaves, field workers and immigrants who came to places like Detroit looking for opportunity. These people unquestionably improved the quality of others' lives, while little value was placed on their own.

The album's third track, and first single, 'The Big Three Killed My Baby,' is a power-chord indictment of the auto industry. Jack, whose omnipresent jewelry is made of used auto parts, claims not to be a big fan of cars, nor of the companies that make them. *"Don't let them tell you the future's electric / because gasoline's not measured in metric"* is his way of illustrating the corporate lie: the auto companies have no interest in improving cars or the environment until they find a way to make money from it. They initially planned to put 'Stop Breaking Down' on the b-side of a single with 'The Big Three Killed My Baby,' making it "a whole anti-automotive 45," says Jack. "Then when we recorded it, it came out so good we figured we'd better put it on the album."

 ## I just want to play 'John The Revelator' one more time

'When I Hear My Name' is a super big-beat basher for Meg and a shimmy-shake garage classic with a one-two-three-four-five bop. Listen to the BBC radio session performance of it and you'd swear Jack was singing the later verses in tongues. But watch out for that 13th beat at the end.

'Cannon' sounds like a Detroit history lesson come alive, as in the sound of cannon fire and cannon balls splashing into the Detroit River during some grand battle over the territories. In the middle section, White has injected Blind Willie Johnson's 'John The Revelator,' an important part of most any White Stripes performance you'll see or hear. (An amazing rendition of the pairing of 'Cannon' and 'John The Revelator' can be heard on the first John Peel session.)

White calls Willie Johnson, "the greatest slide player ever." Blinded as a child in Marlin, Texas, Johnson played a spiritual brand of blues, and is considered to be the best of the bottleneck slide guitar players. His recording of 'John The

Revelator' reached wider audiences in 1952 when it was included on Harry Smith's *Anthology Of American Folk Music* (reissued in 1997). But it's most likely that White came by this tune via first-wave Mississippi Delta bluesman Son House, to whom the album is dedicated and who will return again and again in the White Stripes' story. These days 'John The Revelator' is considered a standard, and White joins artists from Taj Mahal to Beck in reviving it.

"I just want to play 'John The Revelator' one more time," says Jack.

'Astro' is a plain ol' garage rocker that conjures the swampy trash-rock of The Cramps – it's also the one where you're most likely to hear Screaming Lord Sutch's 'Jack The Ripper' to the tune of 'Peter Gunn' bust out during its middle break when it's performed on-stage.

Hero Dylan gets tossed into the mix with 'One More Cup Of Coffee,' an outlaw, gypsy tale. In 'Little People,' Jack puts on his best child's voice and gets into the business of mythmaking as he spies a little girl with the red shoes on: *"Hel-lo..."*

'Slicker Drips' (*"nobody to love..."*) could go overlooked except for the extraordinary drum and guitar interplay – which is part of the thrill of a White Stripes live show.

'Suzy Lee' is a bluesy slide guitar, lost-my-girl tale. Johnny Walker of Soledad Brothers sat in on slide guitar for it, as he also did on the album's final chant of isolation, 'I Fought Piranhas.'

"I don't think I'd ever played 'Suzy Lee' before," laughs Walker. "I just winged it on the spot. I guess I came in and played and if Jack didn't like it, he told me and I replayed it."

'St James Infirmary Blues' is the penultimate song on the album. Blind Willie McTell, blues hero to Bob Dylan and Jack, also recorded a version of this song, whose roots lie in the English ballad, 'The Unfortunate Rake.'

"Well folks I'm goin' down to St James Infirmary
To see my little baby there
She's stretched out on a long white table
She looks so good so cold so fair"

"The truth of things, that's what drives us," says Jack. "And this is the truth of what we are. Bodies. Bones. It's kinda humbling." Some would say The White Stripes' truth verges on being death-obsessed – on later albums they devote many songs to blood, bones and body parts.

With this mini-suite of life-in-the-big-city blues, The White Stripes had delivered a made-in-Detroit record that sure rocked hard, but with the kind of focus, intensity and all-around vision unknown to any band that had worked there in at least a decade, if not three. Whether anyone there realized it at the time, there was a new blueprint for Detroit rock in the 21st century, a foundation on which to build.

"Jack especially always seems to have a master plan swimming around in his head," says Janet Weiss, whose own fandom is evidence enough of The White Stripes' power to pull people into their world. "Naivete doesn't breed that kind of ferocious guitar playing. He's a go-getter, a reacher, one of the people who inspires the rest of us to kick some ass."

At the very least, Detroit rock had found a new leader. But it would take some time before the rest of the world would get the idea that something big was brewing in this neglected city. First there was work to be done, another round of touring to do and another record to be made.

As Sympathy label boss Long Gone John has said, "It wasn't until I finally saw them around the time of *De Stijl* that I thought, 'Jesus Christ, what have I got here...?'"

Sweethearts of the blues

A selection of Michigan's movers and shakers:
1: Ex-Gories man Mick Collins, a boyhood hero of Jack White, fronts The Dirtbombs at the Lager House in Detroit, 2002 – The Dirtbombs' line-up includes two bass players and two drummers (one of whom, Ben Blackwell, is Jack's nephew)....
2: Wendy Case with The Paybacks at Hamtramck venue Paycheck's in 1999... 3: Tom Potter led the duo Bantam Rooster.... 4: Tim V. Eight from The Hentchmen on-stage at Paycheck's... 5: Johnny Walker, qualified doctor as well as singer-guitarist, formed blues duo Soledad Brothers with drummer Ben Swank, and they forged an early bond with the Stripes. Always the most politicised among Detroit's Cass Corridor contingent, their name came from Black Panther George Jackson's book decrying conditions in California's Soledad prison.

	1	
2	3	5
4		

Sweethearts of the blues

1: Atmospheric country-rock combo Blanche, fronted by Jack's confidante Dan Miller and his wife Tracee, accompanied by steel guitar, banjo and auto-harp. Jack sang backup vocals on their 2003 single 'Who's To Say'... 2: Jack and Dan in their Two Star Tabernacle incarnation... 3: The Von Bondies, seen here at Shepherd's Bush Empire, London, UK, in early 2002, were one-time close friends and collaborators with Jack and the Stripes. More big-beat Iggy Pop in style, The Von Bondies, led by Jason Stollsteimer (centre), have emerged from the current Detroit-area pack as second-in-line for global fame.

The 'Let's Shake Hands' debut single, first issued April 1998 – note Jack's dyed blond hair.

'Lafayette Blues,' the second single, originally issued November 1998 – a collectors' dream.

1 & 2: The White Stripes, only 18 months old, at Paycheck's, Hamtramck, in March 1999, as part of the *Metro Times Blowout*, a major local music festival... 3: The Dirtbombs' Jim Diamond, on the right of this pic, engineered and co-produced the Stripes early recordings; the drummer in the background here is Whites' photographer Pat Pantano... 4: The Go, fronted by Bobby Harlow, on-stage in late 1999 at Detroit's legendary Gold Dollar – where the audience even helped you dress. Jack is maybe looking across thinking, "That looks like a hard little button to button..."

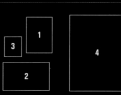

'The Big Three Killed My Baby' single, April 1999 – Jack's swipe at the "shady" auto industry.

The self-titled debut album, released in the US in June 1999, December 2001 in the UK.

1: Jack rocks out, now with his beloved Airline guitar, at the launch party for *De Stijl*, Magic Bag, Ferndale, June 2000... 2: Duetting at the Forum, London, UK, Dec 2001, on The White Stripes' first major European tour – proudly flying the Detroit flag on-stage. *White Blood Cells* mania, plus acclaimed BBC sessions and club dates, had made them UK sweethearts too... 3: Meg at Pier 54 in New York, August 2001.

The second album, *De Stijl*, released June 2000 in the US, issued in Europe in Dec 2001 after the success of *White Blood Cells*. The De Stijl art movement's stark, angular, primary-color designs fit neatly with the Stripes' image. Its biggest single was 'Hello Operator' b/w 'Jolene.'

'Hotel Yorba,' a jaunty tribute to a hometown flophouse, was their first UK hit single, in Nov 2001.

May 2002: The White Stripes on-stage at the Shepherd's Bush Empire, London, during a brief return visit to the UK... In the previous hectic six months they'd played over 50 gigs in a dozen countries, and had also finally gotten to appear on CBS's *Late Show With David Letterman*.

The 'Fell In Love With A Girl' single, Feb 2002 – the one partnered by director Michel Gondry's extraordinary Lego video...

1: Jack in scarifying mode at London's
Shepherd's Bush Empire, May 2002...
2 & 3: The Stripes' growing reputation earns
them one of the main Saturday night slots on the
Pyramid Stage in front of 100,000+ at the UK's
Glastonbury Festival, June 2002... 4: On tour in
Australia, January 2002 – Meg knows these
songs with her eyes closed.

1 & 2: The *Carling Weekend* festival, August 2002, sees The White Stripes playing two consecutive nights in Reading and Leeds, UK...
3: After a relatively quiet few months in terms of gigs (partly due to Jack's *Cold Mountain* commitments and Meg's wrist break), the Stripes kick off the first US dates of 2003 at the imposing Masonic Temple Theatre in Detroit.

'Dead Leaves And The Dirty Ground' was issued May 2001 in the US, 15 months later in the UK.

1 **2** **3**

1 & 2: More shots at Detroit's Masonic Temple, April 2003... 3: One of their biggest thrills to date – The White Stripes performing several Yardbirds songs along with guitar legend Jeff Beck, on-stage together during one of his guest-studded shows at London's Royal Festival Hall in September 2002. Jack and Meg even agreed to play with a bassist for the occasion.

The fourth album, *Elephant*, March 2003.

Biggest hit single so far, April 2003's 'Seven Nation Army' – and yet more enigmatic artwork.

1: Toward the end of 2003 – for instance on the Far East and Australasian tour in October – Jack began wearing black more often, which some ever-eager theorists interpreted as some kind of 'loss of innocence' theme (stemming from his 'death of the sweetheart' statement on the *Elephant* sleeve). Or it could be just that his red t-shirts were in the laundry... 2: Meg had meanwhile begun venturing out from behind the drum kit for her showcase vocal number, 'In The Cold Cold Night'... 3: The White Stripes take a bow at the end of another show... 4: Meg and Jack at the premiere of *Cold Mountain*, Los Angeles, December 2003 – Jack, who has a cameo role in the movie, performed some acoustic bluegrass numbers from the soundtrack at the launch.

'I Just Don't Know What To Do With Myself,' Sept 2003 – not as controversial as the video...

November 2003: 'The Hardest Button To Button' – with another inventive Michel Gondry video.

"Any man with
a microphone
can tell you
what he loves
the most"

Sympathet

sou

**A**nd now a word about rock influences. Rock's most magnificent have historically opened the door for their fans to discover the music (not to mention art, literature and movies) that inspired them. The Rolling Stones took us toward Muddy Waters, Chuck Berry, Otis Redding and Bo Diddley, among others; The Beatles led back to Little Richard, Carl Perkins, Arthur Alexander, the girl groups, Motown and many more. Bob Dylan – considered a 20th century master of original songwriting – also wins the prize as singer of others' songs, from Robert Johnson to Woody Guthrie. We know Neil Young is inspired by guitarists as diverse as Hank Marvin, Jimi Hendrix and Bert Jansch. Bruce Springsteen introduced his massive following to lesser-known artists like Gary US Bonds and Mitch Ryder & The Detroit (yeah!) Wheels.

There is an unspoken agreement among real rockers to preach the gospel of rock, to retell the stories and songs from the earlier rock'n'roll era. The White Stripes, with all of their fervency and belief in the power of rock, are its new ministers. The role call of their patron saints reads like a who's who of popular music, from blues to rock, country and punk: The Sonics, Robert Johnson, Captain Beefheart, The Gun Club, The Stooges, The Troggs, The Gories, The Monks, Bob Dylan, Loretta Lynn, Son House, Blind Willie McTell, Blind Willie Johnson, Dolly Parton, The Cramps, Gene Vincent, Cole Porter, Irving Berlin, The Velvet Underground, The MC5, and Flat Duo Jets.

Dexter (Dex) Romweber, formerly of North Carolina's Flat Duo Jets and now of the Dexter Romweber Duo (with Sam La Resh) says: "I had never even heard of The White Stripes until my drummer Sam told me we had been getting some fan emails from Jack. Sam ran into Poison Ivy from The Cramps and she said something about them, and when we played with X, Exene mentioned them also. All of a sudden there were all these music magazines talking about this groundbreaking two-piece that played stripped-down, primitive punk-blues-influenced music."

The Duo Jets – originally Romweber and drummer Crow, later replaced by LaResh – had recorded rockabilly originals and numbers from the public domain alongside adaptations of songs by artists as varied as Elmer Bernstein, Louis

Prima, Richie Valens, Link Wray and Hasil Adkins. Though the Jets had been together for 16 years and their back-to-basics, timeless, trashcan sound had survived the last two decade's trends, from hair metal to grunge, Romweber says that when the duo broke up in 1999, he found it hard to locate a place for himself and his music. He was left feeling abandoned by the music business, without a booking agent, a label or even a club where he could play. The correspondence with Jack opened up the possibility of playing again.

"The first email message we got from Jack had a very excited tone to it," says Romweber. "He said he was a fan and that he used to have a band before The White Stripes that did a whole bunch of songs off some of the Flat Duo Jets' records. He said that listening to the covers and originals on our earlier records motivated him to seek out the original versions and opened him up to listening to a lot of old early American jazz, blues, rockabilly and surf stuff that he might not ever have known existed.

"He talked for a while about how he really wanted to meet. I have to say we were pretty surprised about the messages from him." Romweber feels there was an extra-weird dimension to the whole correspondence, given that Jack is "such a big popstar" and that Dex is only five or six years his senior.

> Jack said listening to our records motivated him to seek out a lot of early jazz, blues, rockabilly and surf stuff

"We finally asked him if we could play together sometime," says Romweber; but Jack explained that The White Stripes had a policy of not hiring duos as support – something about people's feelings potentially getting hurt…

Romweber wasn't concerned about that: "Our feelings get hurt every day, and we just wanted to play … a gig, any gig."

So on Easter Sunday 2003, Romweber and LaResh finally took to the stage, at the Orpheum Theatre in Boston, as support to their fan's band, The White Stripes. They arrived for their soundcheck and were given the red carpet treatment by the

53

White Stripes' crew – though at first the red-and-white ones themselves were nowhere to be found.

"All of a sudden we started to hear something that sounded like 'Rockhouse' [from the Flat Duo Jets' record *Go Go Harlem Baby*] – it was Jack soundchecking. They played a few Duo Jets' songs. *That* was really tripped out," says Romweber. "They even covered a song off of *Go Go Harlem Baby* called 'Don't Blame Me' in their set that night.

"I don't think our bands sound anything alike, but we really liked them as people. We think they would still be just as good a band without all the hype and matching outfits and rumors of being married or siblings and all that stuff.

"I hope the music business realizes that there are hundreds and hundreds of bands out there in the same vein as The White Stripes that are touring and playing their hearts out to small bars every night all over the USA."

Back in the garage

Romweber belongs to a network of musicians in the international garage rock underground – just some of the innumerable bands that fly below the radar of the mainstream rock press, MTV and the record industry. The White Stripes are sometimes called the world's most successful garage rock band – certainly their relationship to primitive rock and blues qualifies them as a garage act, as do their humble beginnings in the attic (the urban equivalent of the garage). Their choices in vintage gear and recording technology tie them to their sisters and brothers in distorted retro-rock bands. But garage is more than just a kind of music – it's an attitude: tough, cool, untouchable. Even if garage music is an enigma to you, chances are you've still heard some of the highlights from this wide-reaching, bash-and-pop genre. If you haven't, they're worth getting to know.

Most people know '96 Tears' by ? & The Mysterians, garage music's theme song and its biggest hit number ever. It's got it all: the wonky organ melody, the unhinged vocal by an outlaw lead singer, and a swingin' rhythm track. And yes, ? & The Mysterians were from Michigan, and their rock'n'roll classic began life as a local Detroit hit in 1966.

Garage rock has always had its regional strongholds and scenesters: back then it was in the Midwest and West, these days garageland is still in Detroit (with an annex in the UK) and throughout the Rust Belt, as interchangeable line-ups of bands like The Dirtbombs, Ko & The Knockouts, The Paybacks, Soledad Brothers and The Greenhornes, among others, carry out garage rock tradition there and deliver it 'round the world.

You could call garage rock the b-movie scene of rock'n'roll ... the crazy cousin

You could call garage rock the b-movie scene of rock'n'roll – it's the parent genre's crazy cousin. Garage rock isn't about perfection, it's about getting out and doing it. And that's punk – a punk that even pre-dates the roar of Iggy & The Stooges and The MC5.

Garage rock was born in the early 1960s, a fusion of the fuzzy surf guitar sounds of Dick Dale and The Ventures and the white boy R&B of the Kingsmen's 'Louie Louie.' The music got its handle from the garages in the suburbs where young men (only a tiny percentage of women played rock then) were forming bands in ridiculous numbers in the wake of the British Invasion. The Beatles, especially in their film *A Hard Day's Night*, had made being in a band look like such a gas. And The Kinks, Animals, Yardbirds and Rolling Stones were scoring beat-driven hits with riffs that were simple enough for young beginners to learn and play along. Taking their cues from the English rockers' blues-based repertoire, borrowing some fashion tips from style icon Brian Jones, and adding a little feedback and distortion, all added up to garage rock.

Detroit's own Bob Seger System and The Amboy Dukes came up with two stone classics of garage rock: '2+2=?' and 'Journey To The Center Of The Mind' respectively. But for every Troggs and 'Wild Thing,' Count Five and 'Psychotic Reaction' or 13th Floor Elevators and 'You're Gonna Miss Me,' there were probably ten or 20 more groups that languished in a suburban shed.

One of those forgotten bands was Sacramento's psychedelicized Public Nuisance – forgotten at least until a double disc collection of previously unreleased tracks, *Gotta Survive*, was released in 2002, and The White Stripes covered the song

'Small Faces.' In spring of 2003, Jack located ex-Public Nuisance guitarist David Houston and invited him to a White Stripes show in San Francisco, where they played his song.

"He wanted to know all about where we played and I explained to him about the state fair, the teen fairs, battle of the bands, high school dances, community centers, air force bases…" says Houston. "Their version of 'Small Faces' is just so perfect. I can't think of a better band to capture what the Public Nuisance sounded like live. The White Stripes play with an innocent, reckless abandon – just turn it on and go for it. They sound great."

By the end of the 1960s, garage rock was on the wane. While its heart was still beating, the best of the era was compiled by guitarist Lenny Kaye for his *Nuggets* collection. Originally issued in 1972, this psychedelic garage rock primer includes standards of the genre like The Seeds' 'You're Pushing Too Hard' and The Electric Prunes' 'I Had Too Much To Dream (Last Night),' and has since inspired countless collections and series of albums featuring garage rock across the ages. Specialist labels continue to release new garage singles by the truckload, and fanzines and journals chronicle the scene; websites, radio programs and weekend festivals devoted to the form continue to multiply.

As years went on, garage rock became the umbrella under which primitive bands of the trashy, twangy and even rockabilly variety could be categorized. The deathly grind of the White Stripes-influencing Cramps and the bluesier beat of The Gun Club both have a foot in the garage camp – as does New York distortionist Jon Spencer and his Blues Explosion, as well as his former anti-rock outfit, Pussy Galore. Billy Childish has led a one-man crusade to keep garage alive in the UK with his groups from The Milkshakes and Thee Headcoats to its all-girl counterparts Thee Headcoatees (featuring Holly Golightly, who appears with The White Stripes on *Elephant* in 2003). Jack White favorites, the now legendary Mick

> # The White Stripes play with an innocent, reckless abandon – just turn it on and go for it

Collins-led Gories, reignited the garage scene in Detroit City in a big way; bands like The Hentchmen, Bantam Rooster, Rocket 455 and Demolition Doll Rods led the way for a new breed of 21st century garage rockers – most of whom would be featured on the Jack-produced *Sympathetic Sounds Of Detroit* compilation.

Garage has had a profound influence on rock music at large: the late Seventies punk era championed the original garage rockers and some of the classic sides enjoyed second runs and reissues, the sounds meshing nicely with the ramshackle bands of the day. American guitar-rock bands of the Eighties used the feedback-drenched garage sounds to drown out the new wave synthesizer. Traces of garage filtered through Nineties hard rock and grunge. And any time a little boy or girl picks up a guitar or some drumsticks in the attic, the basement or the garage, the spirit of garage rock is alive and well.

Iggy, The MC5 and the Detroit rock sound

The granddaddies of the contemporary Detroit Rock scene, Iggy & The Stooges and The MC5, were the biggest garage bands of their era too – both have provided a steady stream of inspiration to The White Stripes. With roots in blues, old-time rock'n'roll and the relentless grind of the sounds of the city, either one of the bands (depending on which historian you talk to) could be called the original punk rock outfit.

No one screeches a short sharp 'whoop' better than Iggy Pop. Born James Osterberg in 1947, the super-rocker landed on the Detroit music scene when he shot straight out of a trailer park in Ypsilanti, Michigan. Quite possibly the wildest man in all of rock (bodily fluids, peanut butter and silver glitter are no strangers to his stage), Iggy came to be a rock star early – though only a handful of people realized it at the time – as frontman for The Stooges, one of the most influential bands in all of punk rock. With brothers Scott and Ron Ashton on drums and guitar respectively and Dave Alexander on bass, the communal-living quartet, based in Ann Arbor, created a noise that was so far ahead of its time that, 30 years later, even the hardest of rock fans might find their album *Fun House* uneasy listening. Both Jack and Meg claim it as their hands-down favorite.

What The Stooges had going for them, and what The White Stripes share with

57

them, is a beat-driven primitiveness, its heart born in blues. As a teenager, James/Jimmy/Iggy was the drummer and singer for The Iguanas, followed by the bluesy Prime Movers. So in love with the big beat was he that he quit the band and booked on down to Chicago, home of the urban blues, so he could get some more of that stuff. What he found there was inspiration all right – the idea that he could do his own thing. On returning to Ann Arbor he formed The Psychedelic Stooges. The group dropped the Psychedelic, but kept the psych, recording three classic albums before shuffling members and ultimately disbanding (largely due to the massive amounts of drugs three of its four members were taking). After his notorious, gutter-punk walkabout phase, Iggy got it together and went on to collaborate with David Bowie, enjoying a solo career and earning the title of Punk Godfather. He's held that crown throughout punk's many incarnations, mutations and revivals.

In the spring of 2003, The Stooges reformed for a limited string of shows and recorded some songs for Iggy's *Skull Ring* (with Mike Watt, former Minutemen bassist, filling in for the deceased Alexander). In April they shared the bill with The White Stripes at the blazing hot desert concert, the *Coachella Festival* in Indio, California. On August 14th 2003 The Stooges were scheduled to appear in Detroit for the first time in over 30 years. Shortly after soundcheck, the immediate area

If you're in any doubt that the wild and loose MC5 left an imprint on Jack White's rock'n'roll ideal, check 'Ramblin' Rose'

suffered a power outage – the worst in the nation's history – leaving over two million homes in Michigan dark that night and affecting other parts of the Midwest, Canada and New York. The Stooges made up the date one week later. Jack White was there.

If you're in any doubt that the wild and loose Motor City Five left an imprint on Jack White's rock'n'roll ideal, check 'Ramblin' Rose' or the rockin' blues guitar laid down in 'I Just Don't Know.' Spiritually guided and managed by beat/freak John Sinclair from 1966-71, the MC5 – Rob Tyner, Wayne Kramer, Fred 'Sonic' Smith, Michael Davis and Dennis Thompson – ruled the Detroit rock scene centralized at the Grande Ballroom. The band decamped to Ann Arbor in 1968 after the riots and set up a group home, where they made free with a cosmic agenda based on a three-point program of free love-making, drug-taking and rock'n'roll-playing. Originally the name of the

> # The MC5's music – that freestyle combination of rhythm and rock – could only have been made in Detroit

MC5 fanclub, the self-stylized White Panther Party was a pseudo-revolutionary outfit that sank politically but made for a novel accompaniment to the band's scattershot soundtrack. Three rock-solid albums and an in-your-face attitude earned them prototype punk status, while their single-family-dwelling, brothers-and-sisters-in arms communal living arrangement has become a Detroit tradition.

The 1969 debut *Kick Out The Jams*, with its unharnessed hard rock sound, cracked *Billboard's* Top 40, but this would prove to be the band's commercial apex. *Back In The USA* was helmed by first-time producer, rock journalist Jon Landau – it failed to grab the group any more fans in the States, though its sideways Fifties-rock sound earned them a profile in the UK (and of course what Landau could not accomplish for the Five, years later he achieved with another fan of Detroit rock, Bruce Springsteen). The MC5's final album in 1971, the blues-ified *High Time*, turned out to be its swansong.

If the White Stripes' world has three components – melody, rhythm and storytelling – it's safe to say that The MC5 limited its focus even further to concentrate on just one aspect of primal rock: the rhythm. Steeped in the funky drummer sound of James Brown, the band kicked out its own brand of jams with abandon. If nothing else, they gave rock'n'roll one of its most enduring slogans, 'Kick Out The Jams (Motherfuckers).' But it's unfair to say they completely abandoned melody: 'Tonight' and 'The American Ruse' are as much fun as a

59

Chuck Berry classic (he's another inspiration). Maybe it was their third primary influence, space-bound free jazz master Sun Ra, which contributed to the group's inability to pull focus and translate effectively with the masses. Yet it's precisely that freestyle combination of the rhythm and the rock that has earned them a space in the hearts of musicians and music freaks for 30 years now. Their music could only have been made in Detroit.

Baby please don't go: a brief history of British blues-rock

Among the sounds The White Stripes have begged, borrowed and stolen from – though you have to dig a little to detect it – is 1960s British blues-rock, the original back-to-basics movement determined to mine the Mississippi Delta for pure gold. You can draw a straight line from 'Baby Please Don't Go' by Big Joe Williams, follow it to Van Morrison and Them, and shoot it right through Iggy & The Stooges' 'I Wanna Be Your Dog' (a favorite of garage bands everywhere).

'Smokestack Lightnin',' 'I Just Want To Make Love To You,' 'I'm So Glad' – these are some of the best-loved and hardest rockin' songs in the world. And of course, like so many of the greatest songs, these rock-solid pieces were chips off the old blues.

Not only do The White Stripes share a tougher-than-tough, icy cool stance with many of those groups, they share repertoire that's rooted in a love of deep blues. The Sixties generation of British blues-rockers had the original bluesmen as mentors and, as real rockers, they are a crucial link in the chain from the blues to The White Stripes.

Here are a few facts, some widely known and others more obscure, that tie The White Stripes to the blues-rock tradition:-

When Big Joe Williams and Big Bill Broonzy both toured the UK in the 1950s, the British blues-rock wave officially started to roll, but Muddy Waters' appearance in 1958 was the original 'gone electric' performance that shocked purists and inspired young journeymen guitarists to throw themselves into electric blues.

Blues-rock in Britain got off the ground with Blues Incorporated, the bedrock for blues-rock's biggest names. Formed by blues harpist Cyril Davies and guitarist Alexis Korner, an impressive list of players such as bassist Jack Bruce, drummers

Charlie Watts and Ginger Baker and guitarist Peter Green all passed through Blues Inc's revolving doors.

Young Mick Jagger and Keith Richards sat in with Blues Incorporated, as did Brian Jones. The three eventually started their own band, recruiting Blues Inc veteran Watts and bassist Bill Wyman and calling themselves after a Muddy Waters song – and so the Rolling Stones name became synonymous with rock'n'roll.

The Yardbirds were among the most lauded practioners of the blues-rock sound, chiefly because of the guitarists who filtered through their ranks: Eric Clapton, Jeff Beck and Jimmy Page. Shortly after The Yardbirds, and long before he began to wear Armani suits and went unplugged, Clapton was the leader of blues-rock power trio Cream (with Baker and Bruce the rhythm section), a band whose version of 'Sittin' On Top Of The World' we know Jack White learned to play even before he'd heard the Howlin' Wolf original. The Cream has also become virtually synonymous with Robert Johnson's 'Crossroads Blues.'

And that third Yardbirds guitarist, Jimmy Page? Well, we can only guess he's had a tremendous impact on Jack. A live version of 'Ball And Biscuit' in San Francisco in 2003 had Jack directly referencing Page's part from Led Zeppelin's 'The Lemon Song' (which borrows not only from 'Howlin' Wolf's 'The Killing Floor,' but Robert Johnson's 'Traveling Riverside Blues').

White's singing has also been compared to that of Zeppelin's frontman at times – especially on the first Stripes album, before Jack's vocal range expanded with experience and experimentation.

Jack has really got that Robert Plant 'screaming woman' thing honed

"At first you heard that Robert Plant 'screaming woman' thing. He's really got that honed now," Maribel Restrepo of Detroit Cobras told the *Detroit Free Press*. It's an influence that Jack denies – although Plant himself finds that hard to accept, as he told *Mojo* in 2003:

"I love the way that Jack in his interviews says, 'Robert Plant is the thing I least liked about Led Zeppelin.' And I think, well, that's fine, boy, but if you're gonna play 'In My Time Of Dying,' listen to the master … or even to 'Jesus Gonna Make

Up My Dying Bed' from 1930. I tell you, there's no Blind Willie Johnson there. But you know, that sound hasn't really been heard in the contemporary world, in bedsit-college-land, since 1970. So its sudden re-emergence via The White Stripes is like, 'Hey, what's that?'"

So the jury is still out on the Led Zeppelin-versus-The White Stripes question – as it also is on the Jimi Hendrix connection. But c'mon, I say – isn't it obvious? First I direct you to 'Ball And Biscuit' (more on this later). Secondly: White Stripes witnesses from London's 100 Club to LA's El Rey Theater have likened seeing Jack play to what it must have been like to watch Hendrix setting fire to the rock world. In both cases, guitarists in the audiences were either inspired to go further themselves or resigned to putting down the axe forever.

There are plenty of Detroit-British blues-rock connections once you start looking for them. When Eric Burdon visited Detroit in 1966, it was specifically to visit with John Lee Hooker – the pair shared a lifelong friendship rooted in Hooker's visit to Burdon's hometown of Newcastle in the north of England, where the blues rocked the Club A Go Go into the night. Burdon and his Animals shared stages with Sonny Boy Williamson, as did The Yardbirds – both acts worked as Williamson's backing band at various times.

The Animals built a repertoire on a foundation of blues classics. The most enduring impression they made on blues-rock was electrifying the folk standard, 'House Of The Rising Sun,' imprinting it with a yowling blues treatment. As legend has it (and there are plenty of theories on this one), their version fuelled Bob Dylan's idea to electrify his music. Dylan's performance of 'Maggie's Farm' with Mike Bloomfield on guitar at the 1965 *Newport Folk Festival* is an example of what it might've sounded like if he'd taken the electric blues idea the whole way.

Bob Dylan and Jack White

"He's still got it. He still tells it like it is." – WHITE ON DYLAN

Jack White's boyhood friend Dominic Suchyta remembers Jack liked to tell the story about his first concert being a Dylan show. "He said he was four or five and one of his brothers or cousins who was babysitting took him."

Jack's Dylan influence seems to stretch beyond the bounds of average interest, as former housemate Ben Swank of the Soledad Brothers explains: "It's *huge* … He's a big Dylan fan … he covers like three of his songs. [Meg and Jack] both love him. He's both of their favorites."

There is a tight connection between Jack and Dylan, starting with the most obvious points of name changing and self-mythologizing and extending right through their public personae and the country-blues-based repertoire loaded with poetic and encrypted images and phrases.

Covers of 'Lovesick' and 'One More Cup Of Coffee' have both made it to disc (Jack gives similar keyboard treatments in each case but then zaps the former with some heavy guitar), while The White Stripes have included 'Isis' and 'The Ballad Of Hollis Brown' in live performance. Both 'One More Cup Of Coffee' and 'Isis' are from the Dylan album *Desire*, released in 1975 – the year Jack was born.

Bob Dylan has devoted a lifetime to creating the poetry of his songs, in turn helping open the doors and windows of the soul for his listeners. In addition to all kinds of music, he uses classical and contemporary literature for inspiration. As Dylanologists are well aware, Robert Graves' 1940s' book *The White Goddess* muses on the idea that the female is the fount of creativity – with her multiple charms she plays an important role in an artist's life. The White Stripes' inclusion of 'Isis' in their live repertoire is also the closest they get to addressing in song their status as partners/siblings: Isis, the most elevated goddess of ancient Egypt, was both sister *and* wife of Osiris (and in the original mythology is left to reclaim her murdered husband/brother's bones and body parts for a proper burial). In Dylan's song, the narrator marries his Isis on the fifth day of May but can't hold on to her very long. After they part amicably, he can't help but remember that she told him things would be different the next time around – but for now, can they just be friends? There's more to the story of 'Isis,' and for those unfamiliar, I leave you to discover it.

Though Jack hasn't leaned on literature quite the way the young Dylan did,

Meg and Jack both love Dylan ... He's both of their favorites

instead favoring Bob's post-Sixties, more plain-spoken work, most all songwriters take an interest in studying Dylan at some point in their musical lives - though some rockers willfully reject Dylan's songwriting model. Jack has worked overtime on his Dylanology and has chosen to uphold and incorporate its poetic spirit into his work. It's one of the things that distinguishes him from his

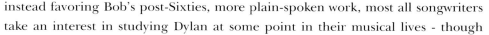

Jack has worked overtime on his Dylanology and has chosen to uphold its poetic spirit

peers in more ramshackle garage and punk rock bands – not that there's anything wrong with ramshackle garage and punk rock.

There are also plenty of similarities between the Stripes and Dylan in the blues and traditional songs they've covered: the 2003 White Stripes b-side 'Black Jack Davey' (an ancient country-folk ballad) was done by Dylan on *Good As I Been To You* in 1992. A partial list of the snatches of country-blues from which Jack and Dylan have both borrowed or reworked include Blind Willie Johnson's 'Jesus Make Up My Dyin' Bed,' and 'Motherless Children Have A Hard Time,' Robert Johnson's 'Stop Breaking Down Blues,' and Blind Willie McTell's 'Dyin' Crap Shooter's Blues.' Dylan's source material could be noted in a separate book – and of course has been, more than once: his connection to pre-war country blues has been documented most expertly by Michael Gray in *Song And Dance Man III: The Art Of Bob Dylan.* Understanding song origins is an important part of contributing to the wider country-blues/rock dialogue, a truth of which Jack seems to be well aware.

The love of old-time music developed as both Jack and Dylan dug deeper into the influences of their heroes. As all good students of music know, all roads lead back to the root. Both artists draw from the deep well of African-American musical heritage; whether it's cover versions of songs by the country blues heroes they both admire (Son House, Blind Willie Johnson, Charley Patton, Reverend Gary Davis, Tampa Red and Robert Johnson, to name only a few) or in the commitment to folkloric storytelling and passing down of wisdom in parable form (dig them liner notes). Even the weirder and irreconcilable aspects of the elder artist's oeuvre –

like his one-time habit of wearing the performers mask of white make-up, or his recent dabbling with early 20th century forms of music from old America (namely minstrelsy) – also show up in Jack's work.

As Jack continued his exploration of Dylan he would have been confronted with the world of *Love And Theft*, the Dylan album named after a book by Eric Lott that put under the magnifying glass the uneasy subject of minstrelsy in America. The songs in minstrel tradition are even older and odder than the country-blues of the Mississippi Delta and the hillbilly music of Appalachia, and many of its songs (think of White Stripes' fave 'Boll Weevil') provide the origins for those later sounds. Such songs also document a hidden history of race relations in America, and you can be sure this idea is not lost on these two fair-Midwesterners from the North country – particularly Jack, whose hometown's current African-American population adds up to over 80 per cent.

Dylan stepped back from direct-action civil rights a long time ago; Jack doesn't even dabble in politics – he claims not to vote or to be interested in such things. Instead it would appear that both songwriters take direction from their faith in God to guide the actions they take. Dylan's well-publicized conversion to Christianity resulted in the gospel recordings *Saved* and *Slow Train Coming*. Jack, raised Catholic, never fails to mention that his favored number, three, is emblematic of the Holy Trinity; he thanks God in his liner notes, and religious imagery is very much at work in his songs.

> He looks at Dylan as an inspiration, as someone who keeps his personal life separate from his career

"A lot of Jack's attitude about his public image, the way he conducts himself in interviews, I think he looks at [Dylan] as an inspiration, as someone who keeps his personal life separate from his career," says Ben Swank.

The common denominator here is elusiveness and mystery. First, there is the use of aliases (Dylan's best known are Blind Boy Grunt and Jack Frost). Both men share the habit of returning to a small circle of loyal friends and collaborators who presumably accept them for who they are and know truths about them that we as fans will never know.

Bob Dylan said he ran away from home a lot, though it turns out he really didn't. Jack said he was the youngest of ten children raised in Mexicantown. Sometimes truth is better than fiction. And as Jack likes to say, sometimes they are one and the same. In blues tradition, the truth is between the lines, buried in epigrams and paradoxes. Dylan, it is safe to say, is a master of the form; Jack continues to practice it, his tales becoming taller, his contradictions more difficult to reconcile (more on this later) as time goes on.

Dylan not only mythologized himself, he told the stories of everyman and of relations with women (again, another book, another time) though at least we *knew* for sure that Dylan had a wife named Sara. In an effort to subsume the individual, Jack has for the most part kept the directly personal out of his work and instead relied on universals. Which is not to say the songs are not derived from personal experience.

Both Dylan and Jack have honored their blues father figure, Georgia 12-string player Blind Willie McTell – Jack with an album dedication and cover versions, Dylan with covers and the song 'Blind Willie McTell' (which some fans believe to be among the greatest in his entire catalog). In turn, Jack's and Dylan's contemporaries have paid public homage to the talent of their peers by covering their work: in Dylan's early career it was artists from Joan Baez to The Byrds and Jimi Hendrix; in the case of The White Stripes, American singer-songwriter Ryan Adams

In blues tradition the truth is between the lines, buried in epigrams and paradoxes

threatened to record a full album of White Stripes' covers; Steven McDonald of Redd Kross actually did that when he added bass to *White Blood Cells*, dubbing it *Redd Blood Cells*, and releasing it over the internet (with Jack's blessing). Tributes to The White Stripes, from a string quartet to electronica versions, have already been issued. At 2003's *Carling Weekend* festival in Reading, UK, Black Rebel

Motorcycle Club performed 'Hardest Button To Button.' The list keeps growing.

And then there are the copycats – musicians who have made Dylan and The White Stripes the source rather than digging deeper for their own roots – plus the boy and girl fans who affect the style and attitude of their heroes. Both practices are a rock'n'roll tradition.

Jack discussed the Stripes' Dylan links in *Mojo*: "Impossible for us not to call him an influence. And

Jack says he finds more to identify with in previous generations than with people his own age

we imagine the same for any musician who truly loves music. Probably no need to tell you why. Our favorite albums are *Nashville Skyline*, *Blood On The Tracks* and *Desire*. Important: do not trust people who call themselves musicians or record collectors who say that they don't like Bob Dylan or The Beatles. They do not love music if those words come out of their mouths. They love record sleeves and getting attention for their hobby, but they don't love music."

Jack says he finds more to identify with in previous generations than with people his own age. Dylan claimed he felt out of touch with his generation too. But classical scholar Graves suggests it's impossible for an artist not to be a part of the times in which he lives – no matter how much he might want to be against his own time or ahead of it.

From the beginning, Dylan adapted folk and blues music to make his own original music. Man out of time Jack uses blues and other rock and country forms for his framework, and has become another unique voice in rock. Like Dylan, the White Stripes have pointed young listeners toward the great old songs and traditions of bygone days. Maybe there is a direction home after all.

Chapter 3

Style and
substance

"The blues is better. Cause it's real. It's not perverted or thought – it's not a concept. It is a chair, not a design for a chair or a better chair or a bigger chair or a chair with leather or with design. It is the first chair. It's chairs for sitting on, not chairs for looking at or being appreciated. You sit on that music."

JOHN LENNON

above: Blind Willie McTell (1901-1959)
right: Meg at the De Stijl *album launch, 2000*

stablishing a work ethic and style built on limitations for themselves, The White Stripes were now prepared to rebuild rock from its roots. For Jack White, American blues was his chair – the seat of creativity that appealed to his need to make rules – and it offered some clear guidelines. The three lines of verse, the first two lines repeating and the third answering (though this rule is just as often ignored) was one way to keep things simple. There is a specific scale incorporating flattened notes – blue notes – that captures the sound of the blues. There is also the tradition of recomposition – a stealing or borrowing – which is fair game in bluescraft. And of course the blues' lyrical language is the stuff of universal consideration: love, death, freedom, spirituality, betrayal and the proverbial search for a home.

The framework for Jack's vision on the Stripes' second album was taken from De Stijl, a stripped-down, geometrically-constrained, back-to-basics art movement established by Theo Van Doesburg in the Netherlands in 1917. Partly based in Theosophical practice, its proponents sought to focus on the spiritual in art through simplification of artistic elements and procedures – creating what Van Doesburg called a "spiritual reality," as opposed to a "natural reality."

"I'd read a lot about the movement at one point and it was just my favorite… because it was such a simple concept," says Jack. "I thought it was almost the equivalent to what we try to do with our music."

De Stijl (it means 'The Style,' and is pronounced 'stayl' in Dutch) established guidelines for artists grappling with the coming of the modern age: they were to limit themselves to using only straight lines and right angles; reject figurative representation and other expressive elements traditionally associated with art; and restrict the palette to the primary colors plus black, white and gray. The De Stijl doctrine served as a mode of purification, the idea being that art would be restored its basic "freedom to follow its own laws" by the exercising of rules and restraint.

Van Doesburg was united with poets, painters, sculptors, architects and writers in the search for beauty and the truth through the contemplation of art, but it was Dutch painter Mondrian who emerged with the highest profile from the group. Mondrian called his own take on De Stijl "nieuwe beelding" – a phrase which has no exact English equivalent, but means something like 'new shaping' or 'new structuring' (though commonly tagged 'neo-plasticism') – and the results are best seen in the artist's vertical and horizontal-lined rectangle paintings which use only primary colors plus black and white. Mondrian eventually fell out with Van Doesburg over the latter's controversial introduction of diagonal lines, and he had effectively distanced himself from his fellow De Stijl artists by 1924, but his work went on to impact the worlds of fashion, decorative arts and advertising. His style later became emblematic of the Sixties mod fashion; its clean lines echoed his art, and dresses and purses were fashioned in the image of his paintings. In the Seventies you might have seen Mondrian design on television's Partridge Family's bus. Today you'll see it in the façade of the Mondrian Hotel on the Sunset Strip in Los Angeles, and the Hotel Bristol in Sheffield, UK (neither accommodation officially endorsed by The White Stripes – at least as far as I know…).

Ultimately the movement would not really take hold as a visual style unto itself (it had similarities and relationships to Cubism, Constructivism and Dadaism), but the De Stijl principles as applied to architecture, and when merged with the work of Frank Lloyd Wright, did develop into what became known as the modern style of design.

We had wondered how simple we could get with people still liking what we do

"The most interesting thing to me, though, the reason I thought De Stijl would be a good name for the album, was the idea that when the De Stijl movement had been taken so far, it got so simplistic that they decided to abandon it in order to build it back up again from nothing," explains Jack.

"We had wondered how simple we could get things before we would have to build it back up again, how simple we could get with people still liking what we do. And on this record we added some piano and violin and stuff, so I thought it fit kind of perfectly – that structure, that building it up. In the same way, we always wear red and white at our shows. It's kind of like our colors. We always do everything that way to kind of keep order. And that philosophy is reflected in the De Stijl movement."

71

De Stijl, the second White Stripes album, was made entirely in the living room at the house on Ferdinand – by now called Third Man Studio – and mixed at Jim Diamond's Ghetto Recorders in Detroit, "at the turn of the century," as the liner notes inform us. A devotion to the blues was still worn on the White Stripes' regulation white shirtsleeves. From the original 'Hello Operator' to the Son House tune 'Death Letter' and Blind Willie McTell's 'Your Southern Can Is Mine,' the blues were given pride of place in the running order: front, center and last. Traditionalists could easily scan the back cover in a record store and deem this record blues-worthy just by the track listing. The three elements – melody, rhythm and storytelling – steeped in blues tradition, were once again present. Garage and the old-time/Tin Pan Alley sound were also represented; a new addition was a strain of gentle pop songcraft, with a lighter touch than on the first album, and a few flourishes including the aforementioned violin, along with bass and harmonica on one track each.

Art, rock, blues and Beck

Certainly there are artists in every medium who understand the value of getting back-to-basics. The Dadaists who preceded and intersected with the De Stijl clan struck out not only against traditional concepts of art but at societal conventions. The Fluxus group of artists in the Sixties was also a collective of rebels with a cause to upend tradition, celebrating the spontaneous and simplifying the notion of art. The Dogme filmmakers who emerged in the Nineties use minimal equipment – again following the creed of creativity through restraint – to deliver artfully crafted films, often with a none-too-subtle agenda. And most certainly Seventies punk rock was a form of breaking it down to build it up again. A reaction to what rock had become in the mid 1970s – an over-produced, over-budget, drug-addled dog and pony show – punk returned rock to its roots, its three chords and upsetter spirit. Instruments reduced to a basic minimum. Do-it-yourself was the battle cry.

In 1997 when The White Stripes were working out their thing in the Ferdinand Street attic space, the DIY idea was in effect. They'd recorded four songs at home, the rest at Ghetto Recorders. By the time *De Stijl* came around, Jack had outfitted the home studio with just enough gear to record the entire album there. Then, back-to-basics in place, The White Stripes were ready to engage in upsetting rock's status quo by taking the seemingly counter-intuitive action of establishing rather than breaking rules.

Like their forebears in artistic rebellion, The White Stripes had reasons to rage against the machine – or at least against circumstances from which to rise above through music. The world right outside their door, Detroit City, was an example of big business and government failure displayed in sharp relief. The soundtrack to that world – whether it was Motown, or the strain of violent, misogynistic or mindless hip-hop, or hepped-up techno – didn't speak to them; nor did it provide any solutions to the problems at hand. Rock at large was unappealing, in need of an overhaul. Alternative music had worn out its welcome earlier in the decade and was now being served up warmed-over (alternative to *what*? was the question of the day) in a million different indie-and alternative sub-genres from emocore to electroclash. By the late Nineties, the goliaths of alternative rock – U2, R.E.M. and their spawn Radiohead, none of which owed any real debt to roots rock anyway – were trading in the kind of high-ticket industry machinations and production values that had forced punk rock to happen in the first place. There was nowhere to go but back.

"I like the rules. When the rules are in place it's beautiful to follow them or break them, but if there's complete ignorance of the rules then it's just unhealthy anarchy. I like Nirvana but after that we just had to deal with all these watered-down rulebreakers," explains Jack.

When punk turned into new wave turned into alternative turned into grunge turned into countless types of new metal and hard-rock, about the only place The White Stripes were going to fit was indie-

I like the rules. When the rules are in place it's beautiful to follow them or break them

rock. No thanks. Indie-rock had become the bastion of the shoegazer, the pathetic, the hopeless and the loser. Its leading lights, Pavement, Sebadoh and Guided By Voices were, let's face it, becoming predictable. In contemporary art and rock, there was a 'pathetic' movement afoot in the early Nineties, spearheaded by indie-rock kingpins Sonic Youth, whose 1992 album *Dirty* marked the apex of a trend. There was nowhere to go but down, into complete despair. Pathetic rock's poster children Nirvana ceased to exist with the suicide of Kurt Cobain in 1994. Nirvana had waged a mini-war on rock, which had resulted in a punk rock renaissance and its commercial acceptance. After Cobain's death – although some rockers heeded his admonition that Corporate Rock Still Sucks (Jack and Meg appeared to be among them) and took his story as a serious cautionary tale about money, guns, drugs and fame – it didn't stop the copycats who would spend the rest of the decade bludgeoning grunge into a new form of heavy-handed hard rock. But there was one lone voice left in commercially successful alternative rock that may have attracted the ears of The White Stripes.

Beck Hansen was born in Los Angeles on July 8th 1970 (five years and one day before Jack). These days you could call him and The White Stripes contemporaries and friends, but back when Beck's hip-hop/talking blues/bottleneck-slide hybrid 'Loser' topped the charts, Jack was still working in the upholstery shop.

Steeped in Latino culture and raised in a lower-income neighborhood among artists (Beck's granddad was part of the Fluxus collective, his mom a habitué of Andy Warhol's Factory), Beck reopened a cultural exchange when he borrowed from the Latino genre, hip-hop and fine art to make his music at a time when US rock fans were swept up in the white suburban phenomenon of grunge. Like White, surrounded by Mexican-American and hip-hop influences, this white boy started to sing the country blues. In Beck's case the songs of Son House and Mississippi John Hurt were what first opened the door to the blues for him.

In Beck's case the songs of Son House and Mississippi John Hurt opened the door to the blues

"I got into playing blues when I was 15, playing slide guitar and listening to every Mississippi John Hurt and Son House record," says Beck. "I lived that music for years, and had no inclination or desire to ever pick up an electric guitar or be a part of any dominant musical cultures at the time … It's not like I'm usurping this stuff because it's suddenly cool – I've just gone where gravity has pulled me musically."

The young singer-songwriter-guitarist immediately became a latter-day blues interpreter of the non-Budweiser-blues variety. Sure, Nirvana tried it with Leadbelly's 'Where Did You Sleep Last Night,' on the 1993 MTV *Unplugged* appearance, but there hadn't exactly been a run on Leadbelly records at the local Tower Records before that. Nor did Beck's US top ten hit 'Loser' with its country blues slide guitar part launch a full-on revival. But just like a blues song, just like an old Bob Dylan song, 'Loser' – with its refrain of "soy un perdedor," derived from streetwise California Spanglish – hit the mainline: anyone who was meant to get it (and then some) got it. And that sound had reached the top of the charts. That had to be encouraging for anyone who loved blues, who loved rock, who loved words and who needed to believe that there would be life after grunge.

Beck immediately became a latter-day blues interpreter of the non-Budweiser variety

The fire under the blues had been turned up again. Record collectors were abuzz regarding the imminent reissue of *The Anthology Of American Folk Music*, edited by Harry Smith. The quadruple disc set had previously been a catalyst of sorts for the early Sixties folk and blues revival and the bible from which the movement would pull its scripture. Some of its recording artists – Sleepy John Estes and Mississippi John Hurt among them – would enjoy revived careers. In the late Nineties, a new generation was about to rediscover the collection's magic for the first time as its original owners awaited its return to print in digitized form. But musicians and music historians had already returned to this source material for inspiration with what seemed like a vengeance.

White Stripes favorites Thee Headcoats, fronted by Billy Childish, had recorded Blind Willie Johnson's 'John The Revelator' in 1989; noisy Bay Area traditionalists Rube Waddell did too. Tucson blues duo Doo Rag were waging mayhem on the songs of Mississippi Fred McDowell, Sleepy John Estes and Muddy Waters in 1994. New York's Jon Spencer Blues Explosion didn't really play the blues at all, though they did have a hand in spreading the word on living Delta bluesman, R.L. Burnside.

"You have no idea what the hell he's singing about," says Von Bondie Jason Stollsteimer of Spencer's brand of blues. "Bell Bottoms! The Blues! Explosion! I have no idea what the songs are about, but I think the music is awesome." He also points out that Jon Spencer's group prior to the Explosion, the scuzz-rock Pussy Galore, was the one that had inspired Detroit garage rockers.

Jon Spencer's scuzz-rock Pussy Galore had inspired Detroit garage rockers

Indie-rock just wasn't ready for a full-on blues explosion; the next generation spent the remainder of the Nineties learning more about the old songs and preparing the ground before Jack White could play his beloved 'John The Revelator' one more time, this time for a worldwide audience.

Beck, with his hip credibility and stealthy bluesmania, had already started to sneak source material into his own sound, contributing to the groundswell. He might throw down 'John The Revelator' in concert, but generally he didn't let the blues banner fly without gussying it up in one of his post-modern pastiches (although he would dig deeper on his lesser-heard *One Foot In The Grave*, and later reference blues-isms – as on his 'Nobody's Fault But My Own' a play on Blind Willie Johnson's 'Nobody's Fault But Mine').

When Beck began performing 'Grinnin' In Your Face' in the early Nineties, he would've been the highest profile Son House revivalist among contemporary indie rock musicians at the time. Today, of course, his association with the songs of Son House, Blind Willie Johnson and the blues has been eclipsed by Jack White, though the two are friends and are known to hang out and sit-in with each other. As years went by, Beck turned his attention toward folk, R&B and just about any other music you can think of to continue to create his own unique patchwork of sound and visual presentation that drew from Fluxus-style Happenings, among other things, for inspiration.

Jack's pre-White Stripes association with Johnny Walker and Ben Swank, who were working out their pre-Soledad Brothers two-piece blues thang in nearby Toledo, was an assurance that younger musicians were finding new ways to incorporate the old sounds into fresh work, without the benefit of a major label or high-tech equipment or any real means of support. The idea that so-called black music from another era could not be played 'authentically' by young white men was never even a consideration for the musicians working in the densely African-American populated Rust Belt.

"Admittedly white people have a bad track record playing the blues," says Swank. "Obviously it's been co-opted by the fanny-pack blues crowd. But that's just education and being able to tell what's soulful and what's wanky, Stratocaster crap."

"We have people tell us all the time, 'I don't like blues but I love you guys.' And we say, 'You're listening to the wrong blues,'" laughs Walker.

"At the time we were coming of age and getting into music, there wasn't anything of substance out there. Whether we were aware of that or not, maybe we were looking for something deeper, that had some tradition and some feeling to it," explains Swank.

"My aunt gave me a Hound Dog Taylor record when I was 18," says Walker – and he took it from there. He recalls coming across an abandoned warehouse in Ohio filled with 78s.

"There are some old record people around that still have a bunch of stuff like that… 78s, 45s, old music equipment – it's a good place to be for all things junk," says Italy label boss Dave Buick. "Walking around my house or Jack's house, you'd probably be able to pick up on that – that it's a good place for junk.

"Doo Rag was a huge influence. Their first CD is 20 songs, a homemade deal, and it's all Fred McDowell songs – really traditional music – these songs you know and love, and they were

Music isn't a museum piece. It should always be changing. If it's not, it's not worth paying attention to

completely messing them up, making it completely their own. Those guys were amazing. And Beck's *Stereopathetic Soul Manure…*"

"...Of course the Gun Club preceded that," notes the elder Walker. Not to mention Led Zeppelin, and Cream, The Rolling Stones and more before them, all masters of their own type of blues appropriation but all of whom at different times caught flack from purists when it came to the white groups' claim to the blues.

"It's a damn shame," says Walker. "But shame on anyone who would say something like that to people who were taking something that's old and trying to do something new with it, expanding on it. Music isn't a museum piece, it's not static. It's dynamic and always changing and should always be changing. If it's not vital, it's not worth paying attention to."

Let's build a home

It's safe to say that *De Stijl* is one visceral album, pumped by a heart of rock'n'blues; it's a favorite of the four White Stripes albums among the hardcore fan legion. From the top's 'You're Pretty Good Looking' (with its pure, now, pop/childlike point of view/Kinks-style, sexually ambiguous rock set to chunky chords) to the bottom's Captain Beefheart-like squonk of 'Why Can't You Be Nicer to Me?' there wasn't really anything on the first album that would've prepared listeners for this new kind of kick blasting forth from the primativist couple.

'Let's Build A Home' is perhaps The White Stripes' most primitive and definitive statement on the subjects of homebuilding and rocking. It begins with the voice of a little boy reciting a Christian children's rhyme.

"That's me when I was six or seven," explains Jack. "My older brother and my mother were taping that. It was some sort of religious song. I didn't sing it right. It should have been, 'I wish I had a little red box to put the devil in, I'd take him out and punch-punch-punch and put him back again.'" (In fact if you listen closely he says "a little red box to put my best friends in"...)

The song kicks in with one of Jack's best Michael Jackson/Iggy Pop whoops, and then:

"Some bricks now baby let's build a home
Some bricks now baby let's build a home
C'mon...!
Awlright...!"

This deceivingly simple song would end up having mega-importance in the Whites' repertoire, from its show-stopping vigor to its talk of bricks, baby, and the all-important home. The devil's in a box, the bricks are red; from 'Let's Shake Hands' to 'Let's Build A Home' we need to know where this story's going to go. (Collectors, please refer to the first Peel Session for the best-ever performance; on the second session 'Let's Build A Home' nicely segues into the Soledad Brothers' choogling 'Goin' Back To Memphis,' a now-regular part of the song in the live set.)

The other gemstone on *De Stijl* is 'Death Letter.' Packed up, suitcase in hand, on down the road, baby on the cooling board – what a picture. The images come courtesy of Son House; 'Death Letter' was recorded for his historic 1965 sessions. In the hands of The White Stripes, this number written with one man and a guitar in mind sounds like there's a full band in the house with all of its rhythmic pushes and pulls. To date the song has developed into something way more than what the studio version offers (again, check Peel Session one to get the idea).

There are nights when 'Death Letter' is quite simply astonishing, the interplay between Jack and Meg a showcase for what just two can do together. Degrees of tempo and mood fluctuate wildly from night to night: sometimes it intros somberly, almost in slow motion, other times it barrels full-steam towards the crashing finish. Sometimes it has a frenzied middle section and other nights it goes without, instead a verse of House's 'Grinnin' In Your Face' to finish it off. But always it ends with the feeling that, tonight, they have conjured the spirit of the dead gal, if not House himself.

Born Eddie James House Jr, sometime between 1898 and 1902 in Riverton, Mississippi (right next door to hallowed bluesground Clarksdale), House was among the original big three Mississippi Delta bluesmen – alongside Charley Patton and Willie Brown – whose brand of blues was absorbed first-hand by a young Robert Johnson and by generation after generation of musicians preachin' the blues.

In 1930 House traveled to Grafton, Wisconsin, to record for Paramount Records – home of many a blues recording of the era. He cut the female-positive 'My Black Mama' and his magnetic 'Preachin' Blues,' two performances legendary in their force, but not especially popular at the time. Whether it was the death of

Patton or the Depression or both, House was hit hard and returned home to Mississippi – although not for long. In the early 1940s, musicologist Alan Lomax (following on the folk-archiving work of his father John), was excited enough by the Paramount recordings, and his discovery that House had influenced Robert Johnson and Muddy Waters, to go to Coahoma County to find him. Locating him living on a plantation, Lomax paid two visits there to record House's spellbinding brand of picking, plucking and testifying for the Library Of Congress. House then relocated to upstate New York, and this time he would stop playing for 20 years.

He re-emerged during the 1960s folk revival, appearing at the *Newport Folk Festival* in 1964. It was his sessions recorded the following year that yielded his now familiar, fervent versions of 'Death Letter,' 'John The Revelator' and 'Grinnin' In Your Face.' He retired from live performance and recording in 1969 and died in Detroit in 1988.

By now even the casual listener or reader has gleaned that House is a monumental influence on the Jack White method of music making. His otherworldly, National slide guitar and mournful moan sing like a prayer of desperation to the lord himself. House found himself caught between the blues and a career as a preacher and, lucky for us, he chose music. Of course his notorious weakness for whiskey and women played a role in his ultimate vocation as well. Part of House's appeal is the ferocity with which he delivers his blues – it's easy to picture him at the pulpit.

As he put it himself: "To tell the truth, I was brought up in the church … I was called to preach the gospel. This is the truth, it's not a lie … You can't take God and the devil together, cause them two fellows, they don't get along so well together. You got to turn one of them loose. Which side do you think the best?" This quote comes from a live performance now available on a DVD titled *Masters Of The Country Blues: Son House & Bukka White* (another powerful, percussive National steel artist, same vintage). It's likely that The White Stripes have seen this performance by House, which projects the bluesman's other-worldly presence on to an otherwise ordinary soundstage. In their nightly performances of 'Death Letter,' Jack and Meg do their level best to capture some of the spooky blues magic conjured by the original Delta bluesman.

Jump now, if you will, a few tracks back on the *De Stijl* blues-train to 'Hello Operator,' the Sympathy single from the album (overshadowed for some by the campy cover of Dolly Patron's 'Jolene' on the flipside). 'Hello Operator' is a number that stands tall in The White Stripes' tower of song. This is the one that helped more than a few folk to board The White Stripes' blues-fuelled locomotive, and it's the one guaranteed to catch the ear of anyone doubting the duo's blues guts – another solid fan favorite. It was in fact the song that, two years after its initial recording, attracted the attention of the A&R department at the band's American label; and live, it's a no-fail crowd-pleaser. Any doubt about Meg's ability is cast aside when it becomes readily apparent that what she might lack in technical skill she more than makes up for in swing factor. Jack meanwhile screeches his can't-pay-the-phone-bill blues. It's only track two and The White Stripes have distilled themselves for you: a little bluesy, a little angry, with a beat that's simple, an oscillating guitar that's fierce, and a vocal which tells a story in a frustrated rasp:

"Hello Operator / Can you give me number nine?
Can I see you later? / Will you give me back my dime?" ...
"How you gonna get the money? / Nobody to answer the phone!"

The song may be a nod to 'Sissy Blues,' performed by Mother Of The Blues, Georgia's Ma Rainey:

"Ah, hello Central / It's 'bout to run me wild
Can I get that number / Or will I have to wait awhile?"

Who knows if it was intentional? Who cares? It's as good a protest song as 'The Big Three Killed My Baby.' Meg taps the sticks in time to the clickity-click of a dead phone line; The Payback's John Syzmanski blows some harp on the outro. Jack grinds a little 'Are You Experienced?' out of the last guitar bits as he stretches to hit the campy high notes.

"Find a canary / A bird to bring my message home"

So now that he's got one, 'Little Bird' is a creeping slide blues about caging up a bird and, erm, disconnecting the phone. The riff is slow and sexy, a little Pagey and fitting for this tiny, slice of scary. Preaching the word – to birds. It's the first time we hear Jack play the slide on his own, with no Johnny Walker sitting in.

"Slide is my one true love," says Jack. "I enjoy the smoothness it gives you, and it's so much more expressive than standard playing ... I know this will sound stupid, but when I play a pedal steel, it feels as if it was the instrument I was born to play. I'm so scared to buy one, though, because you may never see me again..."

'You're Pretty Good Looking' is hardly indicative of the sonic array of places the album journeys, but it's certainly a time-trip in itself. The line, *"But your back is so broken / and this feeling's still gonna linger on until the year 2525"* reminds this listener of the 1969 junk-pop hit 'In The Year 2525 (Exordium & Terminus)' by the forgettable duo Zager & Evans, which mused on the changes the next eight centuries would bring and what God might have to say to his people at the end of 10,000 years of civilization. According to the song, the forecast was not good. (But of course I've digressed wildly here – see *www.denisesullivan.com* for further extrapolations on arcane White Stripes-related knowledge.)

'Apple Blossom' is one of those old-time, minor-key piano songs that are an ongoing part of the Whites' repertoire, this one with a German-cabaret feel – particularly when it's sung live in all its varying accents (delivered with the same mania that sometimes accompanies 'St James Infirmary'). As Jack said at the time: "On this new album ... we're getting more into old melodies ... Kind of a 1930s feel to things, with piano and stuff." A supernatural melody tapped out on piano, 'Apple Blossom' conjures the good-old days while recounting the bad old days of a girl in trouble who's in need of a rescuer. This is a role that Jack's narrator (in this case he's slightly lecherous and sinister) likes to play from time to time. He'll show up later in 'I'm Finding It Harder To Be A Gentleman' and 'Little Acorns' – mourning the loss of values, good manners and chivalry in contemporary society.

'I'm Bound To Pack It Up' reveals yet another side of The White Stripes – namely Jack's knack for sophisticated and sensitive pop melody of the folk-rock variety, the type in which Paul McCartney specializes. Lyrically, the narrator's ability to empathize with his love's loneliness as he "packs it up" may be a very large clue into the working relationship of Jack and Meg White but, then again... that's just a guess.

For all the fuss about having no bass, there is a stand-up bass on this track, while Paul Henry Ossy sits in on electric violin. Meg uses a shaker and floor tom – very Moe Tucker.

'Truth Doesn't Make A Noise' uses the same shades that color the Stripes' version of Dylan's 'One More Cup Of Coffee,' except it's bones instead of the valley that lies below. Part 'Leave My Kitten Alone' and part anger at the singer's own mishandling of what sounds like a very complicated situation. Maybe this is one of those songs where the truth is the opposite of what is actually being told. Hmm. The couple would also begin to perform Loretta Lynn's 'Rated X' (later released as the b-side of 'Hotel Yorba'), a more concise story of a divorcée run down by everyone in town as a home-wrecker when in fact it is she who is heartbroken.

'Sister, Do You Know My Name?' is as a forlorn school-bus blues, as the title implies – it would appear to be the precursor to 'We're Going To Be Friends.'

'A Boy's Best Friend,' a dark slide blues, betrays an interest in music outside the big, bluesy primitive beats and old-time songs – a taste of what The White Stripes might sound like with an orchestra, or a combo with some massive firepower. It's a deep and slow moan for mother with a vocal melody that's pop-rock sweet: "I just don't fit in this place," sung in the sing-song of a misfit whose only friends (besides his mother) are his pack of dogs and cigarettes lined up next to him. This lead may be even more

If it's too good or if it's too fun or it's too enjoyable, just forget it

enjoyable than Jack's solo slide debut earlier in the record. All this talk of loving the slide and never playing it is similar to the idea in the song: the phone's plugged in and on again but it's something he'll "never use, never fear."

Jack's been quoted as saying, "If it's too good or if it's too fun or it's too enjoyable, just forget it." A medical professional might label that kind of thinking as obsessive or compulsive – but of course I'm not a medical professional.

From tracks ten through 13 the blues rule, as the record indulges in pure garage stomp, from the bricks-and-mortar pièce de resistance 'Let's Build A Home' and the stone-age garage punk of 'Jumble Jumble' (with its French-language telephone conversation intro) to the Beefheart-like 'Why Can't You Be Nicer to Me?' The White Stripes covered Captain Beefheart & The Magic Band's 'Party Of Special Things To Do,' 'Ashtray Heart' and 'China Pig' on a special one-off EP for Sub Pop in 2000. To date, the appeal of Captain Beefheart has eluded this particular rock fan (along with, as far as I can tell, the majority of the female gender), but it's worth mentioning for those who don't know that Don Van Vliet, the artist formerly known as Captain Beefheart, in his past incarnation as a musician was a one-time blues and garage-rock associate (witness the nugget 'Diddy Wah Diddy' – not to be confused with Manfred Mann's 'Doo Wah Diddy,' please). These days, Van Vliet lives in Northern California and works as a painter and sculptor.

The album had a pull for people seeking a whole new take on rock'n'roll

De Stijl's magic was not only in its music – though at the end of the day that's what really matters, of course. The album, and The White Stripes themselves, had a pull for people seeking something, perhaps looking for a whole new take on rock'n'roll that was fresh, exciting and pure – something that would redeem alternative, indie and hard rock and elevate them from the depths to which they had sunk.

If you've been listening to rock long enough, it usually takes more than a poster or sleeve to ignite interest in an album; but there was something going on with those pictures and throughout the album's package that drew me closer to The White Stripes. Maybe those De Stijl artists were onto something with their color theory and limitations and breaking down of things to essential elements in an effort to create perfect harmony and communion with the divine. I definitely felt like there was something on that record waiting for me to hear, and clearly there was – I wouldn't be sitting here writing this if there wasn't. I had to have it.

Inside, the booklet was sprinkled with photo reproductions of the designs of De Stijl artists Paul Overy, Gerrit Rietveld, Theo Van Doesburg, Georges Vantongerloo and Vilmos Huszar. Who were all these people? I wanted to know more – I needed to know more…

The images were interspersed with what appeared to be at once amateurish yet artfully contrived photos of Jack and Meg alongside their respective instruments – their very own visual trademarks: Meg and her candy-striped bass drum; Jack and his red Airline guitar and Peppermint Triple Tremelo speaker cabinet. Comprising three rotating Leslie speakers, with a spinning red-and-white peppermint logo in front, the Triple Tremelo was designed by Jack and wired up by Johnny Walker – who admits to some technical problems in its construction: "It blew a lot of speakers before it was working right. It had another design flaw as well: it weighs about 300 pounds."

The must-read thank yous, liner notes and dedication, similar in approach for two albums running, could now be referred to as customary. The White Stripes had confirmed they belong to the elite class of musician who take every part of the presentation seriously. In the Bob Dylan tradition, clues to whatever the writer was thinking about, or dreaming about, were dropped into these album-jacket missives. They provide a guide to the listening experience, a pathway towards unraveling the mystery that was becoming the White Stripes' world.

A portion of the liner note reads: *"When it is hard to break the rules of excess, then new rules need to be established."*

Here, The White Stripes officially establish themselves as rulemakers, a habit that would absolutely become their trademark as we got to know them better. The note is penned by Jack (signed 'III') and elaborates on the esthetic principle of simplicity. I could elaborate, but I won't.

The dedication shout-outs went to De Stijl designer Rietveld, as well as to Georgia giant McTell. The first thank-yous once again belong to God and family. It's probably time to introduce God as a major player in the White Stripes' story, as it would appear that a higher power is a source of inspiration for much of what they do. Their God figures in the stories and the songs (*"and I'm bleeding and I'm bleeding and I'm bleeding right before the Lord"*), the imagery (a detail of Michelango's Pietà sculpture inside *White Blood Cells*), and the demeanor (good, nice), and in the creation of their art (so unbelievably great, you wonder if they just may be getting a little outside help).

More common in country and R&B music than in rock'n'roll circles, a musician's outspokenness about a relationship to his God may find him fans and foes; it has had rockers from Bob Dylan to Brian Wilson to Bono labeled both positively and negatively. When Jack White interviewed Iggy Pop for *Mojo* in 2003, he asked him, "How aware of God were you when you were younger, in this rock'n'roll environment? What about now?" Iggy's God seems to be of the psychedelic variety, while Jack's, like everything else in his world, leans more toward the traditional. The question of Jack's faith – for instance whether being raised Catholic affects his music and his life – is an interesting one, although for now the answer, like God, falls under the classification Unknowable.

There are a few other bits and pieces to The White Stripes' story that also fall into the realm of the mysterious – states of mind and esoteric practice – which the willing student of White Stripe-ology may want to consider, as they seem to pertain to the magic of their music. I'll lay them out here if you want to dip in. If not, that's OK too. The beauty of The White Stripes, and hopefully this book, is that no one is forcing any ideas or teachings down anyone's throat. As the sayings go: Take what you like and leave the rest …Whatever rocks your world.

Black math: color, numbers and alchemy

"Someone will say, 'Hey, why not cause a storm by wearing green one day?' I mean, why? Why would we do that? Wearing red and white has meaning. Wearing green for a day would just be so bourgeois…" – JACK WHITE (III)

The De Stijl artists, in their choice of colors (with their associated spiritual properties), had hoped to create a new world Utopia with their art. *De Stijl* is the album that embeds the alchemical into the musical world of The White Stripes – a relationship that continues to the present. I'd suggest that skeptics definitely skip the next three or four pages.

By the time they made *De Stijl*, the harmonious red, white and black color scheme was already firmly in place – in fact it was even more noticeable than the first time out, by virtue of its continuance. But The White Stripes' use of color is nothing new to rock'n'roll. Jimi Hendrix was interested in color's vibrational pull. He bridged rainbows of hues, from golden rose, misty blue and violet too, to full-blast purple, twisting the everyday language of color (feeling 'blue,' or 'green' with envy) into dreamier realms that associated color with the occult arts. Prince is no stranger to purple's royal connection, though Joey Ramone's passion for the same color is less well-known. Johnny Cash was the Man In Black: when asked to comment on the legacy of Cash, Detroit's Kid Rock told MTV, "When I think of Johnny Cash I see red, white and black."

Jack White's obsession with color pre-dates the Stripes, going back to his days as an upholsterer. "My whole shop was only three colors: yellow, white and black. I had this yellow van, and I dressed in yellow and black when I picked up the furniture and all my tools were yellow, white and black," says Jack.

In the White Stripes' story, the use of the three colors, red, white and black, has some interesting parallels with the practice of alchemy – the form of chemistry from the Middle Ages with philosophical and magical connections – as well as with the creation of fairytales and myth. Ancient alchemical texts note the process of transmutation occurring in stages referred to as melanosis (blackening), leukosis (whitening), xanthosis (yellowing) and iosis (reddening). Eventually, practioners reduced the colors to three – black, white, and red – yellow having been absorbed into the red, the color of desired outcome. The white stone was a tool used to turn metal into silver. Sheesh, I'm glad they didn't call themselves The White Stones.

Alchemy's basic principle of transformation – to turn base metals into gold and to discover an elixir of perpetual youth, and other transmutations of the miraculous variety – was put to great use in fairy tales. The tales' typical one-two-three formulae see its characters through great difficulty (the black), a period of engagement (the white), on through to the desired outcome or "awakening of the soul's final destiny" (the red). Think of *The Three Little Pigs*: in need of shelter from the wolf, after three tries they eventually succeed in building a home that is impermeable to him, and go on to live in peace.

Joseph Campbell, a pioneer in the field of comparative mythology, theorized that all myths are linked to the human psyche, as they express our universal need to explore our social, cosmic and spiritual realities. We are drawn to myths and legends as a way to better understand ourselves. With all of their gruesome and harrowing obstacles to overcome, it makes us examine our own fears, most of them borne in childhood or earlier, as we find our way towards the truth.

The all-important White Stripes use of red symbolizes truth – all that lies beneath. Below the green of the surface and the brown of the soil, red is at the earth's core. It's the color of the depths, symbolizing all that is holy and secret. Mind, body and spirit are the essences of humankind, and in alchemy, red is the color of a distilled element's true essence. It is the color of immortality, the final perfection, as in the Christian tradition that uses red wine to symbolize the blood of Christ.

Red is also the color of ambivalence: just as sure as it will welcome you in with the switch of the on-button, it can signal STOP at the door. Children love red. Hell is supposed to be a fiery red. The Red Badge Of Courage, Jesus' sacrifice: red. Murder, cruelty and the slaughter of man – they would be red too. Intense passion, be it ardor or anger, is coded red. Seeing red, in the red zone, in the red. Coals begin black, they turn white, they turn red. The heart, the American Beauty rose, the healthy glow – they're red. Red is the symbol of the internal, the female, the full moon, the womb.

Their favored color scheme of red, white and black could have a different meaning every day

Depending on which country you're in, and to which theories and traditions you subscribe, The White Stripes' favored color scheme of red, white and black could have a different meaning every day. But it is red, the strongest color of the palette, that is most universally recognized as a symbol for the life force at the root of all human existence. Red is the color connected to the first or root chakra, the energy field of the human body located at the tailbone and connected to our basic needs: food for nourishment, shelter and clothing for warmth and protection – all necessary for a sense of security. The first chakra governs the bones and blood, again essential to general well-being. All things flow and grow from the first chakra. According to ancient and holistic medicine tradition, an imbalance in the first chakra may result in accidents or injury. In 2003, both Jack and Meg suffered injuries to their bones – Meg a broken wrist and Jack a fractured finger – both in places that made it impossible to pick up their chosen instruments.

Blood, bones and home are among the words The White Stripes use frequently in song, from the first album's 'The Big Three Killed My Baby' to 'Seven Nation Army' from *Elephant*:

"And the feeling coming from my bones says find a home"

Have a look at the concordance at the back of the book to see more examples of the use of blood, bones and red – and other key words – in White Stripes' songs.

The big three

"If we're breaking things down, how simple could they be? It seems to be revolved around the number three – songwriting is storytelling, melody and rhythm, those three components. If you break it down but you keep the three components, then you have what songwriting really is, without excess and over-thinking." – JACK WHITE

"From the very beginning, we've organized ourselves around the number three," explains Jack. "There's guitars, drums and vocals. Red, white and black. It's a universally perfect number... People die in threes. Three is the beginning of many. Focusing on it helps restrain us so we can get more primitive and honest."

So what's with the numbers games? Numbers, with all of their magical and alchemical connotations, play a central part in things The Whites Stripes love, from the aforementioned three-line blues song formula, to the numbering system used by Francis Child to catalogue ballads from the British Isles in the 19th century. Discographer Harry Smith similarly organized and numbered folk music of the late 1920s and early 1930s into three categories – Ballads, Social Music and Songs – on his monumentally influential *Anthology Of American Folk Music*.

There are yet more links to The White Stripes and the number three: Detroit automakers General Motors, Ford and Chrysler are officially known in the US as the Big Three. The number three (and Roman numeral III) dot the landscape of the inner sleeve of *De Stijl* and particularly *White Blood Cells*. And we know that it was their third album that introduced The White Stripes to a worldwide audience. The number three is highlighted on the sleeve of *Elephant* too; look and you'll see that even the Es in Elephant have been turned into threes.

Jack is a fan of the Orson Welles thriller *The Third Man*, and has named not one but three of his business concerns after the film: his one-man re-upholstery firm, his home studio, and his record label.

"Three can be translated in so many ways," says Jack. "There's the trinity in Christianity, and objects in the world: a traffic light; a table can have three legs and stand up; or a wheel on a car can have only three nuts to hold it on. There's a definition about that."

Three is the magic number in Christianity, it's true: there are the Three Wise Men and the three virtues, Faith, Hope and Charity. Jesus was crucified and died at 33 – and he rose on the third day. Three is also the key to some of the other greatest stories ever told: *The Three Musketeers*, *Three Blind Mice* and *The Three Bears*. Children's games like rock, paper, scissors and tic tac toe are driven by threes. Third time's the charm, third time lucky, and the genie and his three wishes. Lights, camera, action! Ready, steady, go!

From the very beginning, we've organized ourselves around the number three

Of course long before Christianity, and even longer before the number three made pop culture history, the great mathematician Pythagoras had a numbers theory (or three). Ultimately, mathematics and the sciences parted ways with the idea that numbers carried mystical significance, but it was Pythagoras who laid the groundwork in the area of numerology, the system in which digits correspond to letters and birthdays and are reduced to a single number.

We're going to delve into this in some more detail here, so again, the cynical and humorless may wish to skip this section. But White Stripes fans may be interested in playing along in the great tradition of the rock'n'roll numbers game. Put it this way: if numbers are interesting enough for rockers from Jimi 'If Six Was

Nine' Hendrix to Joey '1-2-3-4' Ramone and Jack White III to consider, it may be worth a quick look for fun.

One of numerology's basic formulas assigns a number to each letter, as laid out in this table:

```
1 2 3 4 5 6 7 8 9
A B C D E F G H I
J K L M N O P Q R
S T U V W X Y Z
```

The numbers assigned to the name MEG WHITE would be: 457 58925. Add all these digits together, straight across, and you get 45. Add those two digits together to get a single figure, $4+5 = 9$ (which is of course three squared).

Do the same for JACK WHITE: 1132 58925. Adding the individual digits together gives 36. Reduce that to a single figure, and what do you get? $3+6 = 9$.

Now do the same for WHITE STRIPES: 58925 1299751. Yep, it's 63. And $6+3 = 9$.

Whoa...!

The trait attributed to the number nine (number nine, number nine) is visionary thinking. The number nine popped up frequently in the life and work of John Lennon. Yoko Ono was a devotee of numerology. Nine also symbolizes truth and integrity.

"There's truth in that music," says Jack frequently of his beloved blues. The 'Seven Nation Army,' the Seven Seals of 'John The Revelator,' and the seventh son of 'Ball And Biscuit' could also be efforts to consort with the lucky number seven. It's generally believed that those engaged in a spiritual or magical practice are looking for something. Is it a way for spiritual beings in a material world to understand the fates? Or just a form of entertainment? These are but two of the possibilities. Did the conditions of growing up in the Rust Belt, and the disillusionment that accompanied it, contribute to The White Stripes' interest in such hidden forces? Maybe. Harnessing some kind of power, any kind of power, in the face of hopelessness seems to be part of their story.

It's certainly part of childhood and growing up, as is exploring the realm of the mystical – until we are conditioned by society to abandon that side of our human nature. Whatever the reasons, like all things in The White Stripes' world, the big three is loaded with possibilities.

The invisible republic

By 1997, the new Harry Smith box (as it's affectionately known) finally arrived in stores again. Eighty-four songs were packed onto this collection of pre-war American music with a focus on the late Twenties and early Thirties. Some of the tracks, like 'See That My Grave Is Kept Clean' by Blind Lemon Jefferson and 'John Hardy Was A Desperate Little Man' by the Carter Family, feature familiar songs and voices in the traditional music canon. Others, like the Hawaiian guitar-infused 'Fatal Flower Garden' by Nelstone's Hawaiians and the African-American-cum-Appalachian mountain song 'Dry Bones' by Bascom Lamar Lunsford, are vital links in the chain of the development of American traditional music, though they are the mostly forgotten vestiges by inhabitants of the old world.

The color-coded (and thoroughly annotated) numerical system employed by Smith while compiling the anthology, based on alchemical formula, proved to be an important tool for others to understand the map he plotted for a forsaken American musical culture.

These songs and voices are the embodiment of the invisible republic – the place where anyone disenchanted with present reality might consider taking up residence – which scholar Greil Marcus identified in his liner notes to the box and explored further in his book *Invisible Republic*. My interpretation of the republic (I'm not always up-to-speed with Greil) is that it's an imaginary land, the place where the mystery of early 20th century America still rages. In that sacred space, we can still dream of what it was like, what it could've been like and what it could still be, even though the present reality of conspicuous consumption, oil wars and reality TV continues to stifle the last breaths of optimism and vitality in the country built on ideas like freedom and free-thinking.

This was how the *Anthology* may have served its fans in the consumer-driven, conformist and tightly clamped-down 1950s – the precise environment that forced the invention of rock'n'roll. It's likely that the old songs, whether it was an antique like 'Engine 143' or The Yardbirds' 'Train Kept A Rollin',' served The White Stripes and newer bands in a mightily depressed region during the late 1990s in the same way.

The White Stripes rebelled against trends in the culture

Caught in a similarly defined, consumer and media-driven national group-think (or not thinking) and living in an era of unprecedented wealth (before the dot.coms dot.bombed), corporate scandals and environmental nightmares, The White Stripes and bands like them rebelled against trends in the culture, the media and technology (some of them didn't have the means for any other option). These are just some of the reasons they may've chosen to roll backward before barreling forward. The White Stripes stopped the clock, and the Midwest was the perfect place to do it, with all of its junkyards and old world architecture, broken big-business promises, and its golden age well behind it. The wreckage was the fuel for the art.

Experimental filmmaker/artist Bruce Conner told Greil Marcus that when he came upon the Harry Smith box in the Wichita Public Library in the 1950s, "In Kansas, this was fascinating. I was sure something was going on in the country besides Wichita mind control." This is just one example of how that record changed an artist's life. (Coincidentally, Wichita, Kansas, has an association with The White Stripes' story too. It's not only a location in the original All-American fairytale, *The Wizard Of Oz* (in which a child takes charge of her destiny thanks to a little magic), it's also a destination on The White Stripes' own red-and-white-brick road, cited in 'Seven Nation Army' as an idealized "no-place-like-home" worth getting back to.)

Whether or not The White Stripes had actually heard all these bits and pieces from Smith's *Anthology* box source is irrelevant – it had done its job. As Smith said before he died, "I'm glad to say that my dreams came true. I saw America changed through music." The White Stripes had received the vision and the source; it was now up to them to pass on their gifts in the best way they knew how.

Your Southern can is mine

Combining the sounds of the old world, the esoteric knowledge of number and color theory, and a back-to-basics credo, the man/woman team harnessed some old blues magic and delivered a mighty fine rock album with *De Stijl*. For all the combined influences and fancy footwork, some things about The White Stripes had decidedly not changed (and I don't just mean Meg's cork-soled platforms, which she wore on the first album cover too). They remained a two-piece and, as far as everyone was concerned, they were a brother and sister act. But there was one change their fans didn't know about, which had occurred since they'd decided to make music together: Meg and Jack's days as a couple were over. They'd recorded *De Stijl* against the backdrop of a recent separation and imminent divorce that.

And yet, even with this information, and in all of the album's diversity, the trashy and tasteful beauty and unique construction of its individual songs, I can't find anything to sufficiently explain the Blind Willie McTell curiosity, 'Your Southern Can Is Mine,' which finishes out the album. Take a deep breath and prepare to read on...

For the character Enid in the Daniel Clowes cult comic *Eightball*, written into the film *Ghost World* (2001) by Clowes and director Terry Zwigoff, the pre-war country blues offers a clever misfit a way out of what she perceives to be her miserable existence. Enid repeat-plays the eerie Skip James song 'Devil Got My Woman' on her phonograph and, as we watch, she is transported to another place and time – the long-gone Mississippi of Skip James. It's a beautiful depiction of what music does, not only for the brooding, ill-at-ease teenager, but for everyone who uses it to get lost in once in a while. What Enid found on that record, purchased at a yard sale from a slightly creepy "pathetic loser," Stanley, was her doorway into the weird old America – a place where life was simpler, devoid of Starbucks and the friends who work in them and bland, post-high school choices like business degrees. 'Devil Got My Woman' was her way out of all that.

"Was it really better back then?" she asks Stanley in another scene, pointing to a derogatory caricature of an African-American buried in his collectables. "Well, it's complicated," he answers.

I'll say it's complicated. I haven't found any of Jack White's words that address any of the contradictions in the phrase "the good old days," while Meg is characteristically silent on the matter.

Pretty much all Jack has to say on the subject of 'Southern Can' is: "We do that McTell song at the end of the record that Meg also sang on. I listened to a lot of Blind Willie McTell while making this record..."

The band had previously issued McTell's racy 'Lord Send Me An Angel' as a single (with 'You're Pretty Good Looking' on the flip) with its roll call of women, some of them "Hamtramck yellow," the others "Detroit brown." Hamtramck is a Polish/hipster neighborhood on the Detroit side of 8 Mile Road, the dividing line to the suburbs. But location and hard-to-pronounce Polish names are the least of our worries here...

"Yeah, it's hard for me to sing like that, about how great I am," says Jack. "One line goes, 'All these Georgia women won't let Willie McTell rest', and I change it to, 'All these Detroit women won't let Mr Jack White rest.' To me it's a joke, 'cos everybody who knows me knows that women don't like me that much. I was toying with the idea that girls are attracted to cockiness, and bad, bad qualities in men. So I feel comfortable with that song, because it's true. Lying is the artistic way of telling the truth. I'm lying, saying, 'Look at me, look at this.' I'm just telling you the truth – in reverse."

No more confounding is this whole truth-in-reverse thing than on 'Your Southern Can Is Mine.' The old-time jug-band version is delivered by Jack on acoustic guitar and Meg on tambourine – and it's the first time we hear Meg sing along on an album.

> *"Lookee here mama let me explain you this*
> *If you wanna get crooked I'll even give you my fist*
> *You might read from Revelation, back to Genesis*
> *You keep forgettin' your Southern can belongs to me"*

White has been rather outspoken about his belief that the two genders have natural roles, that modern times have eroded them, and that the olden days were better days. So what does this song have to say to listeners today? 'Southern Can' is definitely a song about a man and woman – perhaps a pimp and a prostitute – though its players might be exchanged for a master and a slave, or even the North and the South (or is it the South and the North), with the complex historic relationship between the two.

McTell's lyric at least owns up to a moment of self-doubt at one point:
"When I hit you mama I know I make no sense..."

Violence and wrongdoing in blues songs is not exactly uncommon; sometimes it signifies, other times it is what it is. The recurrent thread of violence toward women in the blues was initially answered in song by the female pioneers of the form, and later intellectualized by feminists and scholars. The influence of 'Your Southern Can' is perceptible on Mississippi gal Geechie Wily's 'Eagles On A Half,' recorded in the same era. But whether these songs are depictions of street life or hatred (or likely some combination of the two) the question remains: why, among all the blues The White Stripes could've chosen, did they choose to end *De Stijl* with this one?

The White Stripes are about the music, and we don't want that to be lost

Perhaps there is no black or white here. Just more contradictions. Like Stanley the 78 collector in *Ghost World* suggests, it's complicated. But things were clearly not better back in the day for African-Americans, women and other oppressed groups, and with that we can only hope Mr Jack White will agree.

The coda to 'Your Southern Can Is Mine' is an actual snippet of a studio recording McTell made with archivist Lomax, which illustrates the uneasy relationship between the black musicians of the era, the white audience appreciating them, and the (mostly) ill-equipped media that covered it.

The Stripes haven't had to field too many questions on race – maybe no one has ever asked. The Soledad Brothers maintain that living and playing in an environment fraught with racial tension is a complete non-issue (though to this Californian's eye, the Detroit garage scene would appear to be almost wholly segregated). But The White Stripes have certainly successfully put the kybosh on any questions about their relationship with each other. It would only be a matter of time now before it would come to the world's attention that Jack and Meg were not the brother and sister they'd maintained they were in their public life, but rather a real live couple, a man and woman who had fallen in and out of love, married and now divorced – and all before this bittersweet suite of songs was released. In March of 2001, the *Detroit Free Press* reported that Jack and Meg had divorced one year earlier. When pressed on the matter by the paper, Jack artfully dodged the question.

"Frankly, we're kind of tired with all the attention on the brother-sister thing. The White Stripes are about the music, and we don't want that to be lost."

As if preparing themselves for the questions that lay ahead, they close *De Stijl* with a recording of a man evading a question – an African-American man evading the question of a white inquisitor. Is it a tricky truth in reverse, a red herring, or just nonsense? Whatever the case, *De Stijl* ends with the words of Blind Willie McTell: "Shook up … Still a little sore … No one got hurt."

And that is the end of that.

Chapter 4

Gonna need
a bigger room

"The American South should
be regarded as a holy land by
everyone. Everything that's worth
anything comes from there."

JACK WHITE (to *Sonic* magazine, 2003)

above: Blind Willie Johnson (1902-1947)
right: the Stripes play New York, 2001

Despite his deep conviction for the blues, it seems as if Jack may at one point have been wondering whether his motives were being misunderstood... "The blues is from such a different time period and culture than where I'm from," he was quoted as saying. "Being a white kid from Detroit who was born in the Seventies is a long way from being born black in Mississippi in the Twenties. I'm always worried that playing the blues is going to be misconstrued as me trying to cultivate an image, or that it's going to come across as fake."

For the recording of their third album, *White Blood Cells*, The White Stripes created a new set of limitations for themselves – and they started with the elimination of the blues.

"We completely avoided the blues ... on purpose. The thing was, 'What can we do if we completely ignore what we love the most?' We figured out all the nos, and everything else was fine. We were forcing ourselves so harshly to create something out of nothing," Jack explains.

Changing the face of rock music was the last thing on their minds. After all, this was a man and woman who loved the blues – the people's music of suffering and redemption and survival, its aim no more grandiose than to lift the singer's and the listener's spirit but for a moment. A few choice listeners had already responded to this cool but awkward, beautiful but strange brother and sister who based their sound on a basic and bluesy three-point program of melody, rhythm and storytelling. The White Stripes were doing OK following *De Stijl*.

"… We sold a thousand records. The whole thing was a play on that ... the idea was that the white-blood version of this music will sell more than the true, honest black version," says Jack.

There were yet more guidelines: no outside musicians and no cover songs, no guitar solos and no slide guitar. Just two Stripes, one red and the other white. Instead of doing the expected – something even bigger and bluesier – they amped-down a notch or two, and left behind the things they loved. This style of tough love was getting to be yet another strictly White Stripe ideal. And their sacrifices ended up having unexpected dividends when *White Blood Cells* became a worldwide hit in 2001-2002.

"We tried to keep it as unorganized as possible. We rehearsed for a week and then went to a Memphis studio we'd heard about and recorded for three days. We tried to rush this as much as possible to make [the sound] really tense," says Jack.

Having built their reputation as a super-charged, spontaneous live act that engages in an on-stage mind-meld without the benefit of rehearsals or a set list, the two were keen to recreate that vibe in the studio. They decided on Easley-McCain, a 24-track Memphis recording facility popular with indie-rock bands from throughout the Southern states and across the US. They cut the album live in one room, as was the practice in the early days of blues and rock. And Memphis, with its rock'n'soul history, was perfect – it said White Stripes all over.

Rock'n'roll holy land

They call Memphis 'Home Of The Blues.' It was there, in the early 1900s, that W.C. Handy, the father of the blues, worked as a composer, bandleader and music publisher. Night after night on jumpin' Beale Street he noticed the songs that got the best crowd reaction in all the bars and showplaces were the most primitive, "the ones with no discernable beginnings or endings." He published 'Memphis Blues' (not really a blues at all) in 1903, and the rest is bluesology. 2003 was declared The Year Of The Blues by the United States Senate in honor of the music's 100th anniversary. But as we keep finding, blues history cannot be tied up that handily, and nor can the history of its offspring, rock'n'roll – although there are some facts that are irrefutable.

Memphis is also the birthplace of rock'n'roll, the home of Sun Studios where Sam Phillips discovered and recorded the musicians who changed the face of popular music in the 20th Century. Phillips had an ear and an eye for the most raw and primitive music and musicians he could find; he took a chance on some unknown hillbilly shakers and shouters like Elvis Presley, Jerry Lee Lewis and Carl Perkins. In his stable for talent he carved space for the operatic Roy Orbison as well as for country giants Johnny Cash and Charlie Rich; groundbreakers in electric blues and R&B – like B.B. King, Howlin' Wolf and Ike Turner – all had a home at Sun. The low-budget, raw recordings made there would become known the world over as the Sun sound – the epitome of rock'n'roll.

Far from being a strictly black or white scene, Memphis is a place where people of both colors have made lasting impressions on blues, country, rock and soul or, best yet, some combination of all four sounds – the sound of Memphis Soul crosses all color lines. But that's not to say the races lived and moved in harmony with each other; Memphis is also the place where an American hero, civil rights leader Martin Luther King Jr, was shot dead in 1968. There is a tension in the air that is not so different from that in Detroit.

"Memphis is about racial collision in both directions," says producer and man-about-Memphis Jim Dickinson (he produced *Go Go Harlem Baby* for the Flat Duo Jets, among others). "The rednecks who are playing blues still feel funny about it because they're playing black music."

Memphis is not a particularly elegant or prosperous city, but it stands as a place where some of the greatest music the world has ever heard was made. It's become a site of pilgrimage. Elvis's outrageous Graceland home and Sun Studios are tourist destinations, as is a newly restored Beale Street. Stax-Volt, Hi Records and the musical giants who recorded in town, from Otis Redding to Al Green and Dusty Springfield, are all a part of its history. Add The White Stripes'

White Blood Cells **is shot through with a rare and raw rock'n'roll energy**

recording of *White Blood Cells* to the list of classics made there: shot through with a rare and raw rock'n'roll energy, it is best compared to those pioneering recordings of the 1950s.

"It's very odd for an album to be so popular and sell so many copies when it was only made in three days. It was just two people doing it with all these limitations being put on themselves," says Jack. "It *can* be done. You can record an album that people will connect with, and you don't have to spend a million dollars and six months on it."

To those who'd heard albums one and two, at first *White Blood Cells* sounded like a heavier White Stripes – more metal and more goth – than the two previous primers in primitive. But this was no new direction; it was a logical progression.

"We just let the songs come out the way they come out: one at a time," says Jack. "It'll make a lot more sense than if it has all this premeditation behind it."

It's true that the songs on *White Blood Cells* seem to come from a deep place in the subconscious, the place where some of rock'n'roll's most powerful yet inexplicable phrases are born. Whether it's *"tutti frutti aw-rooti"* or *"he got toe-jam football"* and *"it's just a springclean for the May queen"* – ask the man with the microphone and he'll probably tell you a different story every time. It's almost better if we *don't* know. The power is in the words' mystery; they can mean whatever you want them to mean. Which is probably why the record struck a chord with so many people, particularly coming of agers: *"Shiny tops and soda pops when I hear your lips make a sound..."* Well, *aw-rooti*.

"I always want to create a bridge between us and the listener and I want it to be so that kids want to create for themselves a story or context to the words," says Jack. "An artist does not write down on the edge [of the canvas] what he wanted to say with it, what it should mean."

Dominic Suchyta says he remembers bits of songs from back when he played with Jack; collectors will recognize titles in White Stripes' performances from as early as 1999. 'Now Mary' was circulating in the days of Two Star Tabernacle. Another example is the brooding 'The Union Forever,' which sprung from Jack's obsession with Orson Welles and *Citizen Kane*.

"I was thinking about different things people said in the film. I wrote them down and some of them started to rhyme, so it worked out," says Jack. The song from the film, 'It Can't Be Love, Because There Is No True Love,' an eerie New Orleans-style jazz tune, is played over a very intense weekend party sequence in the film.

I want it to be so that kids want to create for themselves a story or context to the words

"I could never find what this song was about, if it was a Forties song, some jazz standard – I could never find it," says Jack. "I was trying to play it on guitar, and I said a line from the movie while I was playing the chords. And it was like, 'I wonder if I can rhyme that with something else from the movie?' I had a lot of the lines memorized already, and then I went through the film and started writing down things that might rhyme together, that might make sense together."

"I remember watching *Citizen Kane* with Jack a few times in high school," says Suchyta. "I didn't get it or see what he did in the movie … this was also the time where I started to see that he saw things in a different light. In art and performance, he knew exactly what appealed to him and *why* he liked it."

This is Orson Welles

Today of course it's easy to understand White's attraction to Welles, an honest-to-goodness 20th century maverick if ever there was one. Theater, film, radio and television were all arenas in which Welles not only worked but also innovated and excelled. *Citizen Kane* was his visual masterpiece. It changed the way Americans made movies and watched them. Its influence on pictures at the time and over time is immeasurable. And its message – that capitalism and success could perhaps lead to spiritual impoverishment and the failure of emotion – seems to have had a significant impact on the way Jack White does business. Remember, his studio and label's name, Third Man, is also named for a Welles picture, *The Third Man*.

"Orson Welles is such a big idol of mine, I love that whole auteur aspect."

Welles is primarily remembered for his directorial work on cinematic breakthroughs like *Kane, The Magnificent Ambersons* and *A Touch Of Evil*. He directed and starred in his epic *Citizen Kane* (1941), a thinly disguised story of newspaper mogul William Randolph Hearst. A quintessentially American business and empire-building tale, Welles imbued every frame of it with time, place and feeling of the Golden Age. His *Magnificent Ambersons* (1942), the story of the fall of a Midwestern family of means, was a

He knew exactly what appealed to him and *why* he liked it

prophetic vision about technology's effect on the environment. *A Touch Of Evil* (1958) featured one of the longest crane shots in modern cinema (filmed not far from where I'm sitting in Venice, California).

As if that weren't enough, Welles was also an actor, a voice-over artist, a part-time pianist, theatrical producer, and a visionary. He innovated artistic concepts that seem as if they were always there – most notably the use of narration in radio plays, and the use of white instead of colored lights in theater production. Some more tidbits? He was raised Catholic and he was known to be a gentleman and a perfectionist when it came to his work. He was said to be discreet regarding his personal relationships and he was known for his integrity. When Jack chooses someone to idolize, he doesn't kid around.

Songs of innocence

Aside from the absence of blues on *White Blood Cells*, this is core White Stripes stuff: the chunky, metal-a-thon 'Dead Leaves And The Dirty Ground;' the breezy folk of 'Hotel Yorba;' the super-charged pop-punk 'Fell In Love With A Girl,' the melt-away sweetness of 'We're Going To Be Friends;' the clever drum-and-voice statement on art-making, 'Little Room;' the doom-saying of 'Expecting;' the homage to *Kane* on 'The Union Forever;' and the completely nuts 'Aluminum' (at one time my favorite song on the album, much to the horror of my loved ones…).

'I Think I Smell A Rat' is the kind of stylized minor-key piano stuff Jack likes to slip in when he's preaching one of his morality lessons. Sometimes when the Stripes do it live, he'll throw in a bit of 'Take A Whiff On Me,' the just-say-no-to-cocaine song once performed by Leadbelly, among others. 'Rat' is among Jack's personal favorites.

"We wrote that the day before we left for Memphis … there was one day when I was home by myself and I played one chord on the piano, and I just kept saying that over and over, 'I think I smell a rat.' And I could never think of anything else to go with it. I loved it because I had this whole thing imagined – that it would go into this swinging finger-snapping thing after that – but I never finished writing it. We had this song called 'That's Where It's At' that we didn't put on the first album… 'All you people know / Just where it's at now / walking down the street with a baseball bat now.' It's about the kids in the neighborhood. We weren't going to use that song anymore, and I played that chord, and 'I smell a rat' popped out again. Meg played it with me and I started singing the lyrics from that other song about the kids in the neighborhood again, and we said, 'This is perfect.'"

'Hotel Yorba,' with its singalong jugband feel/Country Joe & The Fish-style cheer, is a 'Subterranean Homesick Blues'-type rant about that flophouse in Jack's old neighborhood. The band tried to film a video for the song there but were turned down by the hotel management and had to find another location.

'They wouldn't let us in," remembers Jack. "They thought we were from the IRS or something. I guess we just looked a little too respectable to get a room there. The funniest thing was we were sitting out in the van saying, 'Man, we can't get in, I can't believe this,' and just then NPR did a review of our new album [on the van radio], saying, 'Here's the new song, 'Hotel Yorba.'' They started playing it, and we were just laughing."

The track 'Little Room' has become a literal meditation on Jack and Meg's creative dilemma.

"If you're a great painter and you're just painting in your room and all of a sudden someone sees it, then they're all, 'This is great! You're a genius! Let's have a show.' So they have a show and everyone goes nuts. Then they're like, 'OK, let's have another show,' and now your inspiration isn't from where it used to be when no one knew about you. How do you keep your inspiration? If you actually are doing something good, how do you handle it?"

'Expecting' is about destination: in this case Toledo. "People don't exactly go there on vacation. The girl in the song was sending me to do things for her, like run an errand … which probably wouldn't be fun," explains Jack. Toledo, Ohio is only about 60 miles from Detroit and, if you remember, is home to the White's friends the Soledad Brothers.

The cheery and naive 'We're Going To Be Friends' is about walking to school with new pal Suzy Lee (there she is again) and becoming fast friends. Imagined scenarios about what young life *could* have been for him are at the foundation of Jack's childhood songs. "I like writing about that. I write about it a lot, actually having friends in grade school and having a girlfriend or something back then when you really wanted it," he says.

'I'm Finding It Harder To Be A Gentlemen' is one of the album's great odes to the golden days. "I'm just interested in knowing, what is the correct way to act?

What is your mind telling you? What is your body telling you to do?" The song neatly sums up a young man in the modern world's confusion as to whether to open the door or not for his young lady.

"To keep a relationship going is constant work, you constantly have to fuel that fire to keep it alive. A lot of people disregard the rules and say, 'If you don't like what I do then forget it.' I think that's wrong, I think people should always be working on themselves," says Jack (and opening the door for your girl is a good place to start).

The stomping 'Dead Leaves And The Dirty Ground' was another one of those songs left over from the early days. "Sometimes there are songs that get put aside until it feels right to do them," says Jack. It starts out with feedback… Go! A riff as big as Led Zeppelin and a tale as goth as all get-out. Dead leaves. Dirty. Ground. Soft hair. Velvet tongue. Sun went down.

This is one of those ultimate make-of-it-what-you-will numbers: I feel bad when the sun goes down too. I also love "*If you can hear a piano fall you can hear me coming down the hall;*" Beck's artist granddad Al Hansen had a performance piece called *Yoko Ono Piano Drop* which involved pushing a piano off a building. And every time I hear the song now, I'm reminded of a night I saw The White Stripes in Los Angeles in 2003 when the piano fell to the floor. But the final verse is the one that goes down as an all-time great piece of White Stripery, no comment necessary. It's safe to say that there are as many interpretations as there are individuals on the planet.

"Well any man with a microphone / Can tell you what he loves the most
And you know why you love at all / If you're thinking of the holy ghost"

When we talk about it now, some say the record cover was eerily prescient – that picture of the couple up against the wall, the painted red, brick wall. Snow covering the ground, the two wearing their usual, auspicious red and white, they've been cornered by seven menacing figures silhouetted in black. Turn the jacket over and the masked marauders are revealed to be camera-wielding paparazzi, dying to take a shot.

And there's the fact that this worldwide hit, *White Blood Cells,* was the third album for the group who, since its outset, had been fixated on the number three, the magic number. Spooky... In interviews, Jack had alluded to an idea that it was the third in a trilogy, which led some to wrongly believe that it would also mark the end of The White Stripes. This is all what you call album lore – fuel for the kind of talk adolescents once reserved for *Led Zeppelin IV* and the cover of *Abbey Road*. Here was rock'n'roll tradition and mystery at work in The White Stripes' favor one more time. Did The White Stripes set out to make a classic? Beach Boy Brian Wilson tells a story that the creation of 'God Only Knows' and *Pet Sounds* was an answer to prayer; in more than one or two rock'n'roll polls that album has been voted the greatest record of all time. The images chosen by Jimmy Page for Led Zeppelin's fourth album were directly linked to the occult. Again, this harnessing of secret knowledge and special power seems to apply to *White Blood Cells* too – though it was just as likely a subconscious effort on the designer's part.

Motor City madness

Before *De Stijl*'s life as the current White Stripes album had wound down and before *White Blood Cells* was released, the Sympathy For The Record Industry label put out the *Sympathetic Sounds Of Detroit*, a collection of 13 of Detroit's finest garage and blues-rock bands (including The White Stripes), recorded by Jack at his house.

"Jack thought it would be cool to invite all of his friends to come up and record on the same equipment, same amplifiers, same drums, everyone give it their best song and see what happens – see what it sounded like. It was really an innocent attempt to do something creatively interesting," says Wendy Case of The Paybacks whose smokin', Seventies-style glam 'Black Girl' opens the album.

The Dirtbombs (which includes ex-Gories Mick Collins on vocals and Jack's nephew Ben Blackwell on drums) bash their way through 'I'm Through With White Girls.' (It may not be considered cool to acknowledge, but it's hard not to notice the fact that Collins – kingpin on the pre-Stripes Detroit garage movement – is practically the sole African-American among his peers.) Other bands called upon included Jack's friends in the super-bluesy Soledad Brothers and the Detroit Rock-juiced Von Bondies, plus the hardworking Detroit Cobras, blues duo Bantam Rooster and White Stripes-inspirers, the garagey Hentchmen.

"Jack's intention in making that record was just to get the most clear picture – something really unaffected. He was very hands-off about it," explains Case. "But the interesting thing was, if you listen there are segues between each song that are just snippets of each band playing off-the-hook blues riffs. And that was something he decided... 'I just want you to play some blues,' and everyone shrugs their shoulders and looks at each other... 'Any kind of blues – just make up some silly blues riff.' It was a really revealing picture of how individual these bands are."

Word had started to leak out that there was something happening in Detroit, but as Jack stated in his liner note, "No suit from LA or NY is going to fly to Detroit to check out a band and hand out business cards." Frankly, ever since Seattle in the late Eighties and early Nineties, it had been a long time since record label representatives had scoured the hinterlands in hopes of uncovering the next big thing. Chicago had a spell in the limelight, but since the mid-Nineties rock movements had gone more international (thanks to developments like Britpop and electronica). And to tell the truth, the people who do those jobs at record labels rarely, if ever, wear suits; and they only hand out business cards in the movies. Jack knew that – what he was saying was that he knows the Man couldn't care less about Detroit. And so yea, he was right, no one was coming.

But despite this, Detroit bands kept rising up and making their ways out of the garage rock ghetto. The Von Bondies were looking to be the next group to emerge from town. It didn't hurt that Jack frequently named-checked them as a band that

Word had started to leak out that there was something happening in Detroit

was among his favorites from his hometown; he had also completed producing their full-length debut, *Lack Of Communication*, due for release in the summer.

"When I was in the studio, the thing I was most freaked out by was my voice," says Von Bondies singer Jason Stollsteimer. "The Gold Dollar didn't have monitors, you couldn't hear yourself sing. And at practice we didn't have a PA so I just yelled. So when I was singing in the studio, I had to hear myself back and I'd be so freaked out. Jack helped me through that, 'cos he didn't have a stereotypical voice either. Not many people use vibrato any more, but for some reason it's really easy for people in Detroit."

It's difficult to listen to The Von Bondies and not think of The White Stripes and vice versa. Stollsteimer says instead of it being a problem for either him or Jack, for a time it worked in their favor as young, like-minded musicians.

"If you get two people deep-down alike, it can be a problem," says Stollsteimer. "But in the studio it was fine. Jack and I would agree, and maybe not everyone else would, but as I wrote all the songs, and he was the main producer, what we said went at the time. It probably sucked for Marcie and Don" (bandmates Marcie Bolen and Don Blum – bassist Carrie Smith was a new member at the time).

"I have tapes from when Marcie and I were in the Baby Killers, before The White Stripes were even playing out that much – like one show a month. You listen to the two voices: they're almost identical. It weirded me out when I first met him. Even the same way we play guitar. The old Baby Killers stuff is almost identical to the style of The White Stripes on their first record. We didn't play blues, we played more Crampsy-type stuff, more Gun Club – except we didn't know who Gun Club was … I hadn't heard of them but Jack said, 'You gotta hear this, this is what you sound like.' If I do a song that's kind of evil sounding, then I guess I do."

The Von Bondies are a little more down and dirty, a little more rawk, and all around a little more like a traditional Detroit Rock band. They rock, but they ain't no White Stripes. But yes, at times Stollsteimer, with his freeform, blues-maniac vocalizing, can summon the sound of the Gun Club's Jeffrey Lee Pierce.

Among all the music that has influenced The White Stripes and the young Detroit bands, the city's famous Motown sound and the mega-watt soul-power of its other R&B artists is not something from which they've ever chosen to borrow.

"I was really into soul, but I didn't know that Nolan Strong or Andre Williams were from Detroit till four years ago," says Stollsteimer. Strong and Williams recorded for Detroit's Fortune Records during the label's 1950s/60s heyday – their styles live on in the raucous sound of the Detroit Cobras. Original rapper Williams could certainly provide a link to that other Detroit artist of the moment, Eminem.

"Everyone knew all the big names of Motown, but I don't know, maybe people are against it because of what happened to the Motown artists. You could run into a guy asking for spare change and find out he was a saxophone player on Motown recordings. It's not that out-of-the-ordinary to meet someone who once worked for Motown who is now homeless or on welfare," notes Stollsteimer.

Ever since the rise and fall of the auto industry, Detroiters have had reason to be suspicious of claims by big business (or even smaller homegrown firms like Motown) that they would take care of their own when so many jobless workers have ended up on the city's streets. The most neglected megalopolis in the US, Detroit remains

It's not out-of-the-ordinary to meet someone who once worked for Motown who is now on welfare

unrecovered from the tragedies that have befallen it – most significantly the violent race riots of the 1960s and the recession of the 1970s. The abandoned inner city is the only one its younger citizens have known; there is very little fuel for hope or reason for belief in change or goodwill there.

As for rock bands from there finding any kind of success, well, the town hadn't yielded much since the glory days of the MC5 and The Stooges and even they had failed to strike gold in their lifespans as bands – no wonder the new bands weren't expecting much. It had been years since there was any international interest in the Motor City as anything but the Murder Capital of the US, so Detroit's neo-blues and garage rockers kept their expectations low as they watched each other's backs. They remained wary of outsiders, preferring to keep it all in the family. But the secrets of their scene could not be withheld from the world forever.

By the summer of 2001, it was official: Detroit had an extraordinary rock scene. And as it continued to attract attention coast-to-coast, and as we as outsiders understood it, Jack White and The White Stripes were at the forefront. Why not? They were the best, and Jack, with his production jobs and visionary idea for his band, seemed to be the most industrious.

The White Stripes had created a real rock noise, all without a manager or a publicist working for them; even their website was relatively new. When was the last time a band had gotten so far without some international super-powers to back them up? This fact alone made some of us root for the Motor City Two even more.

Like most everything they do, The White Stripes had done it the old-fashioned way – by touring. And the positive notice in the press was on the strength of their singles and two independent albums. *Rolling Stone* tipped them early in the year as one of the bands to watch in 2001. This kind of grassroots groundswell rarely, if ever, happens any more in the bottom-line driven record industry.

The White Stripes were doing it their way – with originality, individual flair and integrity. The White Stripes were sticking it to the Man. It was yet another time-honored rock'n'roll tradition which seemed to have been forgotten but which The White Stripes were hell-bent on reviving. Yet another reason to cheer them on from the sidelines.

"I admit that it's difficult to understand how it happened and to really know how we should handle the issue," says Jack. "The institutions we really oppose, which are MTV and commercial radio, embraced us. That confuses me and makes us unsure of what we are going to do. I don't know… only that it is a confused and confusing world in which we live."

The White Stripes did eventually find a manager. In their singular style, they named their lawyer, Ian Montone, their manager – they call him their "lawyerger." Add it to the list of so-called career moves turned upside down (or rightside up?) by The White Stripes.

"You get to a point where you think, 'What's a manager going to do except, when he gets an offer, he's going to call me up and ask me if I want to do it or not.' Is there any point to that?" asks Jack.

That spring, an independent publicity firm, the New York-based Girlie Action, contacted Long Gone John at Sympathy suggesting they represent The White Stripes. The women got the job of getting press for the band as *De Stijl's* final run bled into the release of *White Blood Cells* on July 3rd 2001. The Jack-

The institutions we really oppose, which are MTV and commercial radio, embraced us

produced Von Bondies debut was released two weeks later, both on the Sympathy For The Record Industry label.

The White Stripes had earned a reputation as a young, explosive live and recording act on their own terms; now with a team to back them up, they were ensuring that the new album would be considered seriously by those who consider such things.

But anything we thought we knew about this red and white boy and girl was going to be relegated to the boneyard, as all expectations were about to be blown, big time. What was about to happen next wouldn't have added up on paper. The story of The White Stripes' third album is strictly in the realm of vision and dreams.

Before a note was even heard by anyone, before The White Stripes had harnessed everything that they had, loaded it up into one powerful package and said, "Away we go," it had already been decided – they were the next big thing.

Union Jack

In the summer of 2001, The White Stripes traveled from America to the UK for the first time. They were booked into their first BBC radio session with John Peel in late July. The DJ had come upon *White Blood Cells* in a Dutch record shop and took a chance on it. He liked what he heard ("proper, over-the-top guitar playing, as he describes it"), and began championing the band on his show. He was even more impressed when he met them in person. They went for a meal together before the session, says Peel, and "they wanted to know all about Lonnie Donegan and acts from way back. We talked about Eddie Cochran, Gene Vincent, and I mentioned that Son House had once done a session for the program." Most young bands, Peel points out, are "too cool" to acknowledge such veteran influences. When they got back to the BBC studios, the Stripes launched into both a Gene Vincent and an Eddie Cochran number, which bowled over their host.

The session opened with a wild and loose 'Let's Shake Hands' and closed with an even wilder and looser 'Hello Operator/Baby Blue' (dedicated to John Peel). Everything in-between, from the now completely worked-out 'Death Letter' and the always show-stopping 'Screwdriver' to the finale 'Bo Weevil,' was electrifying. A most enthusiastic Peel invited them for a second session in November.

The *New Musical Express (NME)* followed the first Peel session; the magazine put The White Stripes on the cover for the first time on August 8th 2001. Later that week, the day after their first UK gig, at North London's Boston Arms, the Stripes made the tabloid papers with headlines that screeched *'Is This The Future Of Rock'n'Roll?'* and *'Stripes Are Stars.'* Supermodel Kate Moss was at the gig, and you can bet that was reported too. The dailies followed with stories. Jack and Meg had strong feelings about it all.

"We were really angry," says Jack. "We asked *NME* not to put us on the cover and they did anyway. We honestly thought it was going to destroy us. We thought the English press was going to chew us up and spit us out and we'd be left holding the bag. To be honest, we just wanted to go home."

Jack and Meg had already begun to express concern about the overnight sensation trap, how it might distance them from friends and fans, and were careful to keep things all in the family. Maybe they were thinking of Jimi Hendrix, Kurt Cobain… But with no perceptible alcohol or drug addiction problems, The White Stripes as a unit were better prepared than their rock'n'roll brethren to handle the demands of success. As a self-contained twosome, they had been able to grow and flourish – although they are the first to admit they didn't feel prepared to handle what was coming their way.

> At first it was a worry that things were happening too fast for us

"When we first came over here, we thought it would just be a small thing, a low-key tour, you know, with low-key shows," Jack told the British press. "But then we get here, the shows are sold out and everything is going nuts. Like I said, it just doesn't make any sense. In quite a short space of time we've gone from playing to ten people to 1,200 people out there. That's just insane. That's unexpected to us and, to be honest, we don't really know how to handle that.

"At first it was a worry that things were coming too fast, that things were happening too fast for us. But we made the decision that things were not going to change for us because of it. If this type of success is coming from what we are doing – solely from what we are doing – then we don't need to second-guess it. We don't have to think, 'Oh people seem to like this kind of song so we better do more of them.' We've never been like that. We've never been a one-song band and we've never tried to do the same thing over and over again. The way we've handled this thing is that we are going to stay exactly the same."

When The White Stripes returned home from that first trip, things had been building in their brief absence. Oliver Henry of the Soledad Brothers (and of The Greenhornes) experienced The White Stripes' rise as a friend and observer on the Detroit rock scene.

"I think I was in a clothes store in Chicago and I heard them on the radio, and that's when I knew," he says. "Before anything happened for The White Stripes, Johnny [Walker] would say, 'I got a phone call from some guy in England and they want us to come over – do you wanna go if we get it?' And I'm thinking, 'Everybody says that, dude.' At the same time, people were calling Jack and telling him the same thing.

"I think the mistake people make is they believe The White Stripes were born in a burst of light, and the fragments of other bands satellite around them, which is not the case at all. You know, Meg's tried to explain that to people as well. One of the great things, much to their credit, is that they always mention everybody all the time. I can only speculate, but I can imagine how one would feel a little uncomfortable being told you're separate from your peers."

But the fact was that The Whites were breaking away from their identity as a regional, independent-label garage band and were soon to be international rock stars. And that *did* set them apart from the Detroit rock family in which they'd grown up.

Late in 2001 The White Stripes struck an unusual two-album record deal with V2 in the US which allowed them to retain the ownership of their publishing, their master recordings and complete creative control. V2 had the option to pick up the artists on Jack's Third Man label for distribution (and they did so with new wave noisy Whirlwind Heat). But there was still some business of cleaning the slate with the Stripes' original label, Sympathy For The Record Industry.

Sympathy chief Long Gone John explains that, according to the handshake deal he entered into with The White Stripes, there was nothing either party could rightfully claim as having been lost or gained. Everything was speculative – from The White Stripes' assertion that they had not been paid for sales in excess of 150,000 records, to Long Gone's counter that he had provided them with at least $30,000 worth of CDs to sell on the road. Long Gone returned the band their masters and waved goodbye to all future claim and earnings off the band, and the Stripes called off any threat of legal action and found a new distributor. Clearly the relationship was one that served both parties for the time that it endured. And the time on that meter had expired.

Jason Stollsteimer of The Von Bondies had entered into his band's Sympathy deal for their Jack-produced, super-charged Detroit rock debut, *Lack Of Communication*, fully armed with knowledge he'd acquired directly from the Stripes' experience.

"I knew that when he put the record out, that's it. It might sell a million copies, but when he puts it out there, don't expect anything. We would never see a dollar. I understood that," he says.

The Von Bondies were ultimately handpicked by A&R legend Seymour Stein, an old wave businessman in a suit (famed for signing the Ramones and Talking Heads) who actually made the trip to Detroit and signed the VBs to his reinvigorated Sire Records for a second studio album. The Von Bondies also continued their relationship with Long Gone John, as he released some pre-Bondies material through Sympathetic channels.

"I don't want to delve into this much, because it will never look like anything other than sour grapes coming from me," Long Gone told the *Washington Post*. "The White Stripes aren't my story. I've had so many other bands that are just as important to me. Not as commercially successful, but just as important. I'm on to the next thing."

By early 2002, the critics participating in the annual *Village Voice Pazz & Jop Poll* voted *White Blood Cells* number four for the year (a notch above Radiohead's *Amnesiac* and one below Bjork's *Verspertine*). The debut from New York's pride, The Strokes, ran off with the number one spot, and Dylan's *Love And Theft* took the number two place.

How did it *feeeeeel* to Jack and Meg to be sittin' on top of the world? For most recording artists this would've been the end of a good run; seven months and 100,000 records sold. But for The White Stripes, it was only the beginning of their third album's story. There was still another year of it all to come – the stuff of which music business dreams, and nightmares, are made.

New blood

It was arranged that *White Blood Cells* (same track listing, same red-and-white-all-over cover art) would be re-released in February, Valentine's Day month. The fresh start and muscle provided by a big new label combined with the end-of-year/new year's critical endorsements were to keep the band moving throughout the rest of 2002.

'Fell In Love With A Girl' had been getting airplay on important trend-setting radio stations like KROQ in Los Angeles and Q101 in Chicago. The supersonic song races at breakneck speed – among all the bare and basic tracks that year by bands like The Strokes and The Hives, heralding a return to rock'n'roll on the radio, 'Fell In Love With a Girl' best captured the frenetic spirit of the new punk rock and the frantic sound of early rock'n'roll. A video for 'Fell In Love' gained some of that much-coveted rotation on MTV in March, after the pair had agreed to let Michel Gondry direct a short film to accompany the track.

"When someone brings a Lego sculpture of your head to dinner and says, 'This is what the video's going to be,' you pretty much say, 'That's it, go ahead,'" Jack told MTV News. Gondry used vintage (of course) Legos in primary colors to build images of Jack and Meg.

Gondry's video for 'Dead Leaves' fanned the embers of the couple's one-time romance: Jack is depicted returning from work only to find his house in disarray, his girlfriend gone and his vision clouded by ghosts of the past.

Almost everything the pair does is infused with a chemistry that doesn't seem all that sister/brotherly. As more and more people were introduced to the Whites for the first time, the question of the two's relationship began to be bandied about more and more. When the *Detroit Free Press* unveiled the story of marriage and divorce in early 2001, it was well before the masses had heard of the band; by the time people had, those in the know broke the news to those who didn't. All around the world, you could almost hear the sound of confused little children crying.

In May the couple returned to play a triumphant homecoming gig at the Royal Oak Music Theater in Detroit, attended by family and friends – all of whom had remained good sports about staying mum on the subject of Jack and Meg's shared past. In June, both *De Stijl* and the first album were reissued by V2. The band made an outrageous guest appearance at the *MTV Movie Awards*, performing on a custom-built, candy-colored stage surrounded by red and white clad superfans. By August, they were collecting their video awards at the music television network's annual *Video Music Awards (VMAs)*.

> ## 'Fell In Love With A Girl' helped rocket The White Stripes into a new sphere of sales and success

'Fell In Love With A Girl' captured three VMAs (special effects, editing and the prestigious Breakthrough award), and helped rocket The White Stripes into a new sphere of sales and success.

Jack and Meg attended the ceremony to accept the awards on Michel Gondry's behalf. With Eminem taking home four out of his eight nominations and The White Stripes three out of four, it was not only Detroit's year at the *VMAs*, but in rock in general.

All eyes were on the Motor City now, as the *White Blood Cells* promotion and tour juggernaut continued for the rest of the year, getting more and more surreal as the days flashed by on the calendar.

The band did double dates with The Strokes in August in their respective hometowns. The Strokes' debut, *Is This It*, was released in the UK just one month after *White Blood Cells* (it was two months later in the States), and they too had managed to stay on the road for a year to promote it. Along with The White Stripes, The Hives, The Yeah Yeah Yeahs, and The Vines, The Strokes were credited with returning rock to its basic, primal state (though as pretty boys of privilege, The Strokes are less appealing as rock'n'roll saviors).

Though The White Stripes rejected the tag that placed them at the forefront of a movement, the message in their music, and in that of the other Detroit rockers, was clear: rock'n'roll had saved their lives – or at least given it some kind of direction. Where else was a smart and creative kid from Detroit going to find salvation?

"It is a city which is quite distinct from sunshiny Los Angeles and cultural New York," explains Jack. "It is a city which is constantly grey and dirty, which is clapped out and poor. To which you can add that the weather is extreme, with the most freezing cold of all winters and then the most unbearably hot summers that I can imagine. It is a city which has the worst of everything. Which probably makes you go seeking beauty, wherever you can find it. At least that is what I have done."

Thanks to the White Stripes and the sympathetic sounds from their brothers and sisters, rock'n'roll had a flash point again. Yes, there were rumblings, something in the air, maybe people needed to be shaken out of their stupor. Rock *had* been dead. Boy and girl pop bands passing as youth music? It just wouldn't do any more. Ever since the white-washed rock days of Pat Boone and Brenda Lee, kids were supposed to know better. And all of that rap and metal, strangulated into rap-metal? Played out. That land-of-the-lost, indie-rock? Dead. But The White Stripes know what to do with a corpse – in fact, it's their special area: they are rock'n'roll undertakers. They revived the music and let it breathe again.

With *De Stijl*, the White Stripes demonstrated their versatility, dexterity and familiarity with rock and blues; with *White Blood Cells*, they ruled it. Whether they wanted the spotlight shone on them or not (and they didn't), it wasn't really up to them. Rock fans of all ages were just glad to have the sound of rock back after what had seemed like an eternal hiatus. If The White Stripes and Detroit rock hadn't saved

Where else was a smart and creative kid from Detroit going to find salvation

rock'n'roll like the papers said they had, well they had at least recaptured some of its lost soul.

The Stripes teamed with The Von Bondies for some touring in the UK – though it's safe to say the pairing won't be happening again anytime soon...

"The tour was stressful," says Jason Stollsteimer. And things were to get more stressful over the coming months. At the time Jack was dating Marcie from The Von Bondies: "He's the guy who's bringing us on tour, but I have his girlfriend in my band," says Stollsteimer. "And on that tour she wasn't pulling her weight – which she knows – whooping it up with Jack every day while we were doing all the work. So it became like she wasn't part of the band. And so when we did tell her, he got mad at us. And she should've done it herself. But he liked to have control. And so do I. And so it was constant arguing."

Jack and Jason's subsequent escalating war of words was eagerly charted by the British music press, which didn't do much to reduce tension. (Ultimately the pair's animosity turned violent: on December 13th 2003 Stollsteimer received hospital treatment for injuries sustained during a brawl with White at Detroit's Magic Stick.)

In September 2002 The White Stripes were invited to sit in with guitar legend Jeff Beck for two nights during his retrospective show at the Royal Festival Hall in London; other guests were Mahavishnu John McLaughlin, Pink Floyd's Roger Waters and soul shouter Paul Rodgers of Free/Bad Company. It was The White Stripes' job to perform the Yardbirds portion of the set with Beck: they steamrolled through 'The Train Kept A Rollin',' 'Heart Full Of Soul,' and 'I Ain't Done Wrong,' among others. Anybody with lingering doubts about Meg's qualifications as a drummer may as well grab a slice of the old humble pie now since it's not every day that a rock drummer is invited to play the Royal Albert Hall with a guitar legend.

"We played Yardbirds songs with a Yardbird, and were honored to do so," Jack wrote on The White Stripes' website.

"Can you imagine?" says Jack. "It was unbelievable. It was the most fantastic thing I have done. I really love that he is still that guy who just doesn't care about anything, who wants only to play guitar and nothing else."

The White Stripes were accompanied by Jack Lawrence of The Greenhornes on bass – plenty of players would've loved to have been in his shoes that night.

"If you're gonna do a gig with Jeff Beck and play a bunch of Yardbirds songs, then the first person you think of is Jack Lawrence," says former Greenhorne bandmate/now Soledad Brother Oliver Henry. "We used to do 'Lost Women' … I'll tell you one thing: in almost five years I played in a band with him, that dude never messed up once."

The following month Jack and Meg accepted an invitation to open for The Rolling Stones in Toronto on October 16th and in Columbus, Ohio, on October 20th. When asked to comment on the upcoming shows, Jack quipped something like, "We can't wait to meet Brian Jones." The reality turned out to be a little more mind-blowing. As they were playing, The White Stripes noticed that the band – The Rolling Stones – were watching from the side of the stage. Stripes friend Dave Buick was in the wings too:

"The roadie or the manager was telling Jack that they never watch the band, and they were all sitting there watching the whole time," says Buick. "It was pretty cool… pretty surreal. You read Mick Jagger and Keith Richards saying they're into The White Stripes: it makes perfect sense but at the same time it doesn't."

"The only thing that meant something to us was that we got to be the support act for the Stones," says Jack.

Between appearances with the Stones they were on national television as the musical guests on *Saturday Night Live* (Senator John McCain was the host). You can read that last sentence again, because it's a long way from the attic on Ferdinand Street and the Gold Dollar.

You read Mick Jagger and Keith Richards saying they're into The White Stripes

Maybe that's why, when Jack took time off to act in a major film over the summer, it was kind of played down at the time. It just would've been too much. Now of course most people know that he plays a role in an adaptation of Charles Frazier's American Civil War epic *Cold Mountain*, directed by Anthony Minghella (Oscar-winner for *The English Patient*). It's the story of a soldier who rises from his deathbed but rather than return to the front he deserts and undertakes an *Odyssey*-like journey back home to North Carolina and his true love. One can see why this piece of period romance would appeal to Jack's old-fashioned, Southern-style sensibilities. Jude Law and Nicole Kidman star, and Jack plays Georgie to Renee Zellweger's Ada.

Sting and Elvis Costello were asked to write songs for the project but it was wee Jack who was asked to write, act *and* sing on the set alongside the likes of bluegrass legend Ralph Stanley.

"I went down to Nashville to record the soundtrack, and met all these amazing bluegrass musicians. I wanted to start crying. I thought they'd picked the wrong guy," says Jack. "The whole thing was deeply humbling. I didn't even want to touch an instrument around those guys, I just said, 'OK, I will sing, humbly sing.' Much as I love American folk music, I didn't think that entitled me to be in that world."

Jack had a chance to perform 'Sittin' On Top Of The World,' the song he learned back when he was a kid playing with Dominic Suchyta.

"'Sittin' On Top Of The World' was actually the first blues song I learned to play, after I had heard Howlin' Wolf's version," affirms Jack. He also performed the traditional 'Wayfaring Stranger,' a song he had once done with Dan Miller's band, Two Star Tabernacle.

So here he was, the so-called savior of rock'n'roll, called upon to sing the old songs one more time.

Jack had started the year 2001 like a next wave Sam Phillips, corralling his region's most talented and most primitive and getting them all down on tape. By the end of 2002, he and his 'big sister' had become rock'n'roll stars in their own right thanks to one Little Album That Could.

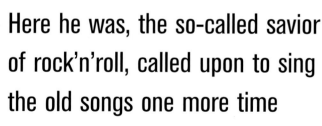
Here he was, the so-called savior of rock'n'roll, called upon to sing the old songs one more time

Everything the couple had come to represent – the colors, the number three, the mythical, the primitive, the anti-technology/anti-corporate agenda, the dark and the light, the longing for the Golden Age and the harking back to childhood, the back-to-basics garage rock – all coalesced on this one bracing and unfiltered rock'n'roll classic. Fifty years after rock's inception, the new rock'n'roll really seemed to be as simple as the old rock'n'roll. And just like Elvis, a white-blood brand of blues had set the world on fire.

What started as a play on words – *White Blood Cells* – ended up a rock'n'roll legend. Not only is the commercial success of the record a great part in the continuing saga of The White Stripes, it is legendary because it seems as if the album will go down as a classic – not just as a 2001 thing.

We can never truly know if it was a plan, a coincidence or divine intervention that led The White Stripes' third long player to become the one that sold the most and connected with the most people. Luck and timing always seem to play a part in the selling of a rock band. But The White Stripes' success is exceptional, partly because it's built on such a raw sound. They've never once sacrificed nor compromised their innate aptitude for primitive rock'n'roll, nor their love for it. Sure, on *White Blood Cell*s they'd abandoned the 12-bar blues on which they'd built their reputation… but was the album entirely blues-less?

The poetry of the blues is as rich as any literary or song tradition. Verse upon verse, blues songs deal with every aspect of human existence, delivered in a form that is warm, simple and familiar, but at the same time elusive and mysterious to the outsider. Blues speaks directly to the audience for which it was intended, in its own tongue, in universal emotions. If blues is simply an expression of the human spirit's ability to look inside, or fly above and rise to a place in the mind where we are all free, then blues is whatever you want it to be. Maybe The White Stripes didn't leave the blues behind at all for their blues-less *White Blood Cells*.

The influence on The White Stripes of the American South's bluesmen (much like that of the American South itself and its role in the history of the US) is integral to who they are, even when they aren't playing the blues. Had The White Stripes not studied the music, and also felt oppressed in their own way, they would not have been nearly as prepared to make and break *White Blood Cells*.

After becoming rock's next big thing, covering so much new stylistic and songwriting territory and doing it well, selling a million records and fashioning an album cover with the lure and lore of a classic, what would the Detroit rock duo do next, now that they had our complete attention? They'd return to the UK to make an album and play a little blues again – of course.

Chapter 5

Going
to Wichita

"Krazy wonders if it's 'love' and we wonder if you
do – and maybe you wonder if we do – and then
again, maybe you're not 'wondering' at all – how
should we know."

GEORGE HERRIMAN, CREATOR OF *KRAZY KAT* CARTOON STRIP

above: country music star and Stripes' icon Loretta Lynn
right: Jack at Detroit's Masonic Temple Theater, 2003

t the beginning of 2003, when asked about his goals and directions, his intentions and plans, Jack seemed to have just one thing on his mind: all he wanted to do was make it out of here alive. He was 27, known in some circles as the year of rock'n'roll death – because Jimi Hendrix, Jim Morrison, Janis Joplin and Kurt Cobain hadn't made it to their 28th birthdays.

"I guess I'm just going to try to get throughout this year without dying…"

He was more than halfway there. But even when he talks of things less bleak and more upbeat, like say his music, Jack's public persona enjoys keeping a lid on the enthusiasm thing.

"We're still happy creatively because we've put so many limitations on ourselves that we live in this little box. Everything else that happens is just extra. We're not living for fame and fortune; we don't think that equals happiness. The trick is not to become satisfied. I'm pushing away enjoyment on a lot of levels constantly. It's tough. If this success is what we'd aimed at from the beginning then we'd probably be excited. But it wasn't. If your dreams come true, what do you do? There's nowhere to go but down."

The White Stripes are not known for their rock star excesses – if anything, they've earned a reputation as being conservative and against all that. Again, it's one of those pieces to their puzzle that make them attractive to a certain type of folk. It's not exactly a moral consideration, rather it seems to be about those limitations – and priorities – with a little consideration for what's cool/what's not thrown into the mix. In the White Stripes' world, conspicuous consumption of anything, from clothes and cars to groupies and drugs, would be entirely… uncool.

"Once you get a little fame, you get drinks and clothes for free. But when you had to pay for them, you couldn't afford them. It makes no sense," muses Meg. It's one of those weird twists of fate that has always confused me too. And what a great example of how, instead of blathering on about nothing and everything, Meg saves up her words till she has a point to make.

"It's an effort to restrain, sure," continues Jack. "We have it harder than anyone else because we set rules. Everyone wants to have fun, and sometimes I wish we were a little bit dumber.

"We're not trying to come off as a say-no-to-drugs band, we're not trying to be judgmental," he says. "Look at your average teenager with the body piercings and the tattoos. You have white kids going around talking in ghetto accents because they think that makes them hard. It's so cool to be hard. We're against that."

That sounds fair enough, in as much as The White Stripes have forged a song catalog that's about one quarter devoted to songs of innocence.

"It's sad to see young kids today – they're sitting around listening to hip-hop or nu-metal, with a Sony PlayStation, a bong of marijuana. This is their life. It's a whole culture. And the parenting is so relaxed about that," he told the *New York Times*. In another interview he asserts, "I stand for the values I feel are right, not those which are in vogue at the moment."

I stand for the values I feel are right, not those which are in vogue

There's something about the tone Jack takes, or at least the way in which he's quoted, that leaves a little holier-than-thou ring around the collar of The White Stripes' otherwise impeccable image. I like to think that the soapboxing is an intentional ploy to separate the wheat from the chaff in the audience. Or maybe Jack has just been asked one too many questions, one too many times.

There was certainly no shortage of White Stripes in the media circa 2002-03. With barely a break in the action after *White Blood Cells*, and leading up to their fourth offering, *Elephant*, there was plenty to keep the presses rolling: the DVD release of the *White Blood Cells* videos, special guest appearances and non-stop tour dates. And word on the forthcoming album was evidently some of the most anticipated music news in recent rock history.

Then the following message was posted on the band's website:

"We have finished the making, mixing and mastering of *Elephant* but won't let it out of its cage just yet. It needs to graze on the plains for a minute. Perhaps it's not what Meg and I think it is. Perhaps it's the worst album we've ever made. Or perhaps we'll all be surprised. We'll see, I suppose, but at the time it was a good feeling, and it may come back and roost forever." JACK WHITE III

Jack later expanded: "This time our limitations were: we're going to another country, we want to finish it in ten days, and we're going to work only on an eight-track. There's a sort of wave with White Stripes records. There were a lot of limitations on the first album, a little relaxing on *De Stijl*, then super-limitations on *White Blood Cells* and then relaxation again – but we're still inside a box that's 100 miles away from popular production."

The box this time was ToeRag studio in Homerton, Hackney, East London. The White Stripes booked in for ten days to the tiny retro studio, owned and customized for minimalist rockers by Liam Watson (a garage-bander and enthusiast himself) who engineered and recorded the sessions. Watson is of the same mind as Jack when it comes to recording technique, so it was a perfect fit.

"Up until 1968, there wasn't a studio in Britain that had more than four tracks, and think about all the great records by The Beatles, The Rolling Stones, and others that were made during that time," the engineer told *Guitar Player*.

We like to be uncomfortable ... You should feel forced to be working on something

"We first heard about ToeRag when a friend of ours from the Hentchmen recorded here," explains Jack. "He was telling everyone how amazing it was. We were kind of drooling ... I don't like those kind of places where the studio is nicely heated and you've got a cappuccino machine and video games to use in-between takes. We like to be uncomfortable ... You should feel forced to be working on something. It feels like school to me and I like that."

Recorded in the spring of 2002 and mixed and mastered in the fall, it hadn't even been a year since their first visit to the UK, and yet the American band felt at home enough to make a record there. From engineer Watson and art designer Bruce Brand, to first-ever guest vocalist Holly Golightly and the songs' talk of tea, biscuits and the queen (plus a cricket bat on the cover), *Elephant* was truly an offering to Great Britain. And even though there was a new record label and a whole pile of money at their disposal to make an album, The White Stripes stuck to their original low-budget, low-tech, highly constrained approach.

"It was just a nice collection of old microphones and staying away from digital equipment," explains Jack, who terms the new technology "disgusting."

"They did have a four-track there that might have been used on 'Tomorrow Never Knows,' for backwards loops and things like that," says Jack. Watson inherited some equipment from the famed Abbey Road Studios, most notable for its Beatles recordings. "You can find studios that have all the same equipment that he does, but they also have all this other modern stuff ... To give you too much opportunity really destroys creativity. If you took an artist you respect and put them in a room with a broken guitar and a two-track recorder, something more interesting would come out of them than if you put them in some fancy LA studio with a million dollars to spend."

The White Stripes are serious when they say that *everything* was better in the olden days...

Elephant's 14 songs are as good a representation of the band as you will ever hear: there's the bluesy 'Ball And Biscuit,' the alchemical garage barrage of 'Black Math,' the sugary 'You've Got Her In Your Pocket' and a solid blast of that hard, ambitious and uptight rock that is uniquely White Stripes: 'Seven Nation Army,' 'The Hardest Button To Button' and 'There's No Home For You Here.'

> # If people asked what the album was going to be like, I always said, 'You're not going to like it'

Like the old joke about the blind man and the elephant, depending on where you touch him, this elephant is whatever you need it to be.

"There was no real conscious thought involved in the different styles. Every album we've done, we've always tried to bring the songs that were written and just force them all into this box and make them work. We never premeditate anything. If we went in and said, 'OK, we want to make a country record or a soul record,' we would just fail miserably," says Jack.

"If people asked us what it was going to be like, I always said, 'You're not going to like it.' That left me free not to think about it any more. The recording experience was actually the best we've ever had," he says.

129

"We're proud we managed to ignore the outside world," says Meg. "Not once did anyone say, 'Which one's going to be the single?' Or, 'Do you think people will like this?' We just did it. A third of it was written right there," she says.

Jack wrote 'It's True That We Love One Another' the same day it was recorded. A garage rocker from way back, Brit Holly Golightly sits in, and is the last voice you hear on the album, ordering a cup of tea, to "celebrate" (just as Blind Willie McTell's conversation rounded off *De Stijl)*.

"I've played stuff with them before," says Golightly, "but this is what they chose to use on their album. There wasn't really that much of a strategy," she laughs. The song is a lighthearted jug-band party song, in part an homage to 'Creeque Alley' by the California Sixties folk-rock scenesters The Mamas & The Papas – and perhaps also another nod in the direction of Willie McTell, whose duets with his wife Kate sometimes featured a similar back-and-forth bantering. Performed by Jack, Meg and Holly, it's a self-referential story of love among musicians. As the connection between The White Stripes and Golightly is longstanding, the joke flowed quite naturally.

"Detroit is not that different from where I come from," explains Golightly. "When you live in a place where all the industry is gone you have to make your own entertainment."

The cross-cultural, mutual admiration society doesn't stop there. Golightly has an association with Sixties rock revivalists The Greenhornes, a Rust Belt band with whom she tours. But she's not counting on her association with any up-and-comers or stars of the region to propel her into a new stratosphere.

"At least more people might have an idea of who I am, but I don't think they're going to rush out and buy the records on the strength of somebody they've never heard of tacked on to the end of someone else's record," she says.

So, we're all wondering, is it really true that they 'love one another'? Where *do* they all stand, since it's they who've joined the melée and asked the question…? I think we can assume that Holly's presence is purely as a comedic and musical foil for this one-off track – but the real, ongoing interest is in Jack and Meg themselves. Does Jack still love Meg? Does Meg still love Jack? At the time of the album's release, the pair were said to be dating other people, their own past relationship still not open for clarification by the outside world. But to believe that the songs on *Elephant* are only from the head, and that there's nothing in them from the heart, would be like saying there is no such thing as love or the possibility of love.

Does Jack use personal experience in his songs? He says yes. Does he bring things from imagination to life? Yes. On the seven-inch sleeve of 'Seven Nation Army' he's pictured in the act of painting a portrait while Meg poses for him in her long white granny dress; on his canvas, there is a painting of an elephant.

"Meg is the most important part of the White Stripes," says Jack. And as such, her role as sister/lover to seventh son Jack has become an important part of the listener's experience with the songs. Just because we're not supposed to let these facts detract from the music – we're not supposed to talk about it, just like that big elephant in the middle of the room – doesn't mean people aren't thinking about it the whole time… It's hard *not* to think about it (and the youngest of fans have a hard time getting their heads around it).

There is a quality of emotionalism to Jack White's songs that seems like it just wouldn't be present if it was anyone but Meg behind that drum kit.

"You know, when I hear music, I just hear the whole thing. I've never been much into picking things apart. It's the emotion of it that hits me, more than anything technical," says Meg. And she speaks for a huge portion of the rock audience who take in music exactly the same way – which is precisely why you haven't read much about amps and guitars in this book.

I don't want people to think the gear is all it takes to get my sound

Even Jack, despite his obvious interest in vintage musical equipment, was at pains to tell *Guitar Player* magazine in mid 2003: "I'm not a gear head – I don't know anything about what makes an amp work … I do pay a lot of attention to making my tone as powerful as it can be … I mean, it's just me and Meg up there, so the guitar has to be strong … I just don't want people to think that the gear is all it takes to get my sound."

Elephant has a new kind of self-awareness and confidence – the kind that comes with experience and a measure of successes – plus it's fearless, effortless and humorous. The elephant might be afraid of the mouse, but if you mess with him, he is capable of destroying everything in his path. The elephant is an animal of contradictions.

"It's how we've seen our personalities through all this," says Jack. "We're powerful and majestic, but also subtle and innocent. Clumsy yet brilliant. Also silent. And the way elephants relate to death is interesting. They get real emotional about it. Elephants bury each other. Other animals would either eat one another's remains or just not care. Elephants care."

Filled with tales of love, relationships and how to get on in a world gone wrong, *Elephant* can be read as an open letter to whomever it fits: you, her, him, the ex, the first girlfriend, the third man… It's Jack singing to Meg, it's Jack in the role of Meg singing to Jack, it's Meg singing (in the voice of Jack?) in the cold, cold night. All is fair in love and everything is possible in the candy land that The White Stripes have so brilliantly constructed – which suits whatever the listener needs it to be.

"I hate irony," says Jack, "particularly when it's used because there isn't any message, or to hide that someone hasn't any story to tell. Just like when someone only spews out a stack of cool words which don't mean anything and then has the gall to call it art."

Gone country

Home sweet home, the simpler days of childhood and the Eden that was: these are among the most beloved themes in the American music tradition, and you needn't dig very deep into The White Stripes' songbook to glean what is at the forefront of the writer's mind.

Born into their intensely decayed urban environment of Detroit, the Whites take us to a necessary make-believe scene of days gone by. The band's presentation as an idealized family – two similarly-aged and liked-minded siblings enjoying life's simple pleasures, seeking the comforts of hearth and home – are themes that have driven their music for at least four years now. Rather than the stark realism and negativity of hip-hop, The White Stripes' candycoated world is one in which the baby is king and home is the idyllic paradise of our dreams: mother, father, sister, brother, the good old days, children at play, a happy, healthy home.

Over the course of four albums and accompanying singles, the words 'home' or 'house' have appeared in White Stripes lyrics at least 40 times, the word 'baby' at least 30 times (see the Concordance at the back of the book for more). The family home theme is straight out of country & western and its predecessor, hillbilly music. Though there is rarely a twang in a White Stripes tune, there are plenty of C&W hallmarks, as in tears in beers (*"a pack of dogs and cigarettes"*) and an emotionality (*"I want to be the boy to warm your mother's heart"*) that you don't hear much in rock music.

The notion that the olden days were golden days may have made its first appearance via the songs of Stephen Foster, widely considered to be the inventor of American popular music as we know it. 'Old Folks At Home' (*"Way down upon the Swanee River..."*), a song transcribed by and credited to Foster but like others of the era discovered to be African-American in origin, is an early example of a song that at once meant different things to different people, but which captured the feeling of being displaced. From slaves abducted from their homeland to immigrants looking for a better way of life here to anyone else reeling from the rapidly expanding and industrialized America in the late 19th century, 'Old Folks At Home' and songs like 'My Old Kentucky Home' and 'Sitting By My Own Cabin Door,' among many others, conjured a vision of a paradisiacal home.

With the invention of the radio in the 1920s, those stationed far from home tuned in to its comforts. The rise of hillbilly music, a combination of Appalachia's sound and imported English/Celtic ballads with a shot of blues, enjoyed its greatest popularity in the 1930s when family singers from the Southern states told their mythical stories of migration from the agrarian, garden-like South to the harsher and colder, industrialized regions of the North. These hard-scrabbling people had learned there was only one institution on which they could rely: family.

The idea of the loving mama and the little bitty baby in American song is borne from the mountain of people's daily lives. Mother, father, aunts, uncles and multiple siblings worked together to keep the operations moving. By tradition, particular care and attention was given to the youngest in the family. These 'little adults' did all of the same things that their older siblings and relatives in the family did, though they were coddled, sometimes literally held in hand, while doing it all. In the words of bluegrass pioneer Bill Monroe, "Back in them days, a kid was babied and patted more than they are today."

The baby of the family would always be the baby... As the youngest of ten, Jack will always be the baby – which might explain why he handles the childlike themes with an unusual precision: from the way the music is based on the simple concept of beat, melody and storytelling, to the way Meg plays ("it's so childlike," enthuses Jack) to the fact that they go for the color red ("Like kids do," says Jack). They have video characters of themselves made of Legos, 'Jimmy The Exploder' and a "monkey jumping on the bed;" Meg literally jumps on the bed in the video for 'Hotel Yorba.' It's a wonder that a cartoon series starring Jack and Meg hasn't been created for television yet: *The Adventures Of The Motor City Two*... Plenty of their fans are under ten; a visit to their internet chat room finds posts exclusively by webbers who are very young (or at least young at heart). Of course older and middle-aged fans find much to identify with too – rock'n'roll helps us stay young – as we find our way home.

As the youngest of ten, Jack will always be the baby

Having twisted these shopworn Americana archetypes, The White Stripes have turned something so old into something so new that it has become virtually unrecognizable. We have a few clues that there is some country ham behind it all: *Elephant*'s cover costumes; the choice covers of Dolly Parton's 'Jolene' and Loretta Lynn's 'Rated X' (both of which Jack sings from the female perspective); Jack's love of pedal steel; his involvement in the Loretta Lynn and *Cold Mountain* album projects; and finally, his association with his old friend Dan Miller of the countrified Goober & The Peas and Two Star Tabernacle, with whom he continues a close collaboration. And though the Stripes themselves come from a town where country music enjoys a relatively sparse audience (the banjo is not generally a friendly sound to the urbanite), they *did* dedicate *White Blood Cells* to country queen Loretta Lynn. But it wasn't until *Elephant* that the band's affinity for country could truly be nailed.

Coal miner's daughter

Dressed on the *Elephant* cover in remnants from the Grand Ole Opry, the higher Meg piled her hair the more she started to strike a resemblance to her heroine, Loretta Lynn. It was Lynn's daughter Patsy (named after country singer Patsy Cline), who brought her mother's attention to *White Blood Cells*. Lynn was so curious that she invited Meg and Jack to her ranch in Tennessee in early 2003; they returned the hospitality with an invitation to Lynn to open for them at New York's Hammersmith Ballroom.

"She'd heard the record and was very happy we dedicated it to her," says Jack. "We sorta asked if there was a chance we could play a show together and she was for it. We did three songs with her on-stage. She's an icon and a genius, I think. It was brilliant playing with her … There could be a relationship brewing between me and her," Jack laughs.

By summertime, he was producing songs for Lynn's next album. "I wanted to cry when I heard these songs. She's still writing amazing songs," he says.

"She's written so many songs, saying it like it is," adds Meg. "Saying things that people didn't dare to say at the time she did it."

Born in Kentucky in 1935, Loretta Lynn didn't sing professionally until 1960; by then she was already the mother of four children (in fact she'd had all four while still a teenager). The beginnings of her career were truly DIY: her husband Mooney bought her a guitar and the pair set up auditions, recording sessions and even delivered her first single, 'I'm a Honky Tonk Girl,' to radio stations nationwide by hand. The result of their collaboration was a Top 20 hit. A string of successful woman-power songs followed – 'Don't Come Home A Drinkin' (With Lovin' On Your Mind),' 'The Pill,' and 'Your Squaw Is On The Warpath' – all of which were written and performed by Lynn. In addition to the solo acclaim, she enjoyed musical partnerships with two country legends, Ernest Tubb and Conway Twitty. She told her own amazing story in the book *Coal*

> I wanted to cry when I heard these songs. She's still writing amazing songs

Miner's Daughter, which was adapted into a film, earning actress Sissy Spacek an Oscar in 1980.

Jack claims to have been a fan of Lynn's ever since he saw the film as a kid – but his real interest in her artistry developed about ten years ago.

"I really think she is the best singer-songwriter of the 20th century. I think she's very underrated," he says.

The Whites have done what they can to increase Lynn's cachet among their own crowd. Jack sat in with her (on 'Louisiana Woman, Mississippi Man' and 'Fist City') when Lynn opened for The White Stripes in early 2003. They recorded a wrangly cover of 'Rated X' (the b-side to 'Hotel Yorba') – the song, about a divorcée, adds plenty of fuel to the fire of Jack and Meg's relationship mystery. And as in their version of Dolly Parton's 'Jolene,' Jack doesn't feel the need to trade the female narrator for a male one – rather he plays the female during Lynn's spoken-word outro:

"Us women don't have a chance
Cause if you've been married, you can't have no fun at all
You're rated X
No matter what you do, they're gonna talk about you
I don't know what to do about it
Just let 'em talk, just let 'em talk, Meg"

The high-pitched male singer is a country/bluegrass tradition; it's what allows him to leave his earthly persona and occupy another's space. Jimmie Rodgers, the Father of Country Music, sung his very first recording, 'The Soldier's Sweetheart,' from the female standpoint. Famous for his other-worldly vocal style and songs of ramblers and gamblers, Rodgers' ability to mix blues, country, and Tin Pan Alley styles (along with humor) was his trademark – as was his yodel.

Born September 8th 1897 in Meridian, Mississippi, Rodgers was raised on the region's blues and minstrel songs, and entertainer Al Jolson. Alternating between his jobs as a railroad brakeman (his nickname is the Singing Brakeman, which is also the name of a 1929 short film devoted to him) and as a tent-show, blackface performer, Rodgers' first professional recording sessions were in 1927 for Victor in

Bristol, Tennessee. 'The Soldier's Sweetheart' and 'Sleep Baby Sleep' didn't fare so well, but his 'Blue Yodel' (also known as 'T Is For Texas') is the song that made Rodgers a star; he became country's first internationally known artist. Sadly, his run was short – he died at the age of 36 from tuberculosis – but his influence on country music was massive: performing singer-songwriter-guitarists from Hank Williams and Merle Haggard to Bob Dylan all point backward to acknowledge their great debt to Rodgers.

It would seem Jack has taken his fair share of cues from Rodgers too. Comfortable in the highest of registers, when Jack's vocals take flight, they offer an escape from the humdrum sound of a regular existence. When he gets high, it usually signals desire, frustration and release all rolled into one (think of the sexual hysteria of some of the wilder versions of 'Let's Shake Hands,' and 'When I Hear My Name'). Jack uses the high pitch to great effect – even using a baby voice in 'Little People' and 'Jumble, Jumble.' Different voices denote different characters in his songs: for instance the compassionate male of 'Same Boy You've Always Known' and 'I'm Bound To Pack It Up,' and the bluesy thugs of 'Your Southern Can Is Mine' and 'Ball And Biscuit.'

On *Elephant's* maxi-length blues jam 'Ball And Biscuit,' Jack comes full circle from the Howlin' Wolf miming of his boyhood to a full-grown bluesman with the king-size heavy vibes of Willie Dixon and rock shaman Jimi Hendrix. The seventh son rap is a tip of the Stetson to Dixon, the third man bit a nod to Orson Welles (as well as a little numbers voodoo). He mumbles and then rumbles like Hendrix (check it at about 3:45). It's simultaneously tense and loose, but definitely as relaxed as The White Stripes get – the song's lazy rhythm taking its sweet time about getting anywhere. Borrowing pieces from here and there, just as in the blues tradition, it's shades of Wolf, Robert Johnson and Jimmy Page.

"I think it has a lot to do with the tunings Jack uses," says Soledad Brother Johnny Walker of the Led Zeppelance. "He plays more in open G, which gives you a voicing like Jimmy Page." (Walker himself is more of an open D and E, Keith Richards-type player.)

Elephant also began the generous practice of awarding b-sides to friends like the Soledads, whose 'St Ides Of March' is on the flip of 'Hardest Button To

Button;" while the double-b of 'Seven Nation Army' went to the spiffy ode to cars, guitars and girls, 'Good To Me' by pop writers Brendan Benson and Jason Faulkner, and the country-opera, 'Who's To Say,' written and recorded by Dan Miller's countrified band, Blanche.

The death of the sweetheart

"We mourn the sweetheart's loss in a disgusting world of opportunistic, lottery ticket holders caring about nothing that is long term, only the cheap thrill, the kick, the for the moment pleasure, the easy way out, the bragging rights and trophy holding" – JACK WHITE, *ELEPHANT* SLEEVENOTE

The *Elephant* album's unofficial subtitle and dedication is to the Death Of The Sweeheart. Jack expands:

"It feels like generally in society, without wanting to be pretentious, it's very hard for the sweetheart or the gentleman to exist nowadays. It's not cool ... The morals of years ago are dying. Parenting is becoming a lackadaisical thing. Parents don't care if kids swear to their face. Kids call their parents by their first name. It's not a world welcoming to the idea of sweetness and gentlemanly qualities. As a teenager, I found you can either hold your chin up and stick to what interests you or give up and like what everyone else likes."

The old world sweetheart who entered the White Stripe lexicon in 'St James Infirmary' stuck around for 'Apple Blossom' and tried to work it out in 'I'm Finding It Harder To Be A Gentleman' has finally given up.

"It's kind of a depressing album," says Jack. "The overriding theme is the death of the sweetheart. That romantic idea just can't seem to exist these days. The entire world is wrapped around sexual ideas, it's become so free-thinking that a lot of the old ideas are lost."

One of the lost ideas he's mourning is the erosion of assigned sex roles. "Those roles are destroyed by mass communication, the internet, television. Men cannot give birth, women can. I think people mistake certain things as being sexist when really it's our own defined nature," Jack says, echoing ideas put forth at one time by his hero Bob Dylan.

I like to think that in his own clunky way, Jack is trying to say that woman, giver of life, is by nature softer, more intuitive and nurturing than man, and that we all could use a little more yin with our yang, especially during hard times, no matter what gender we were assigned.

The pleasantries, the niceties, the manners of days gone by, yep, I miss them too. I say thanks to Jack for saying the latter and giving voice to everyone with concerns about the decline of civilization. But this darned freethinker isn't so sure she likes a young musician claiming to know her defined nature...

"Maybe that's what's good though – the idea of the male and the female on-stage and nothing else. It's two different sides of looking at the same thing. It feels like you can see that. I can feel it on-stage," says Jack.

The White Stripes cut a fairly modern picture of what it means to be men and women, or perhaps sister and brother, in a rock band in the early 21st century. The antecedents for male/female duo acts are impressive in showbiz circles – from Sonny & Cher to Karen and Richard Carpenter – but there are few in rock'n'roll. There is no precedent in rock for a show like The White Stripes'. Who says you can't be in a band with your ex-spouse and succeed wildly? Are we not all sisters and brothers anyway? The White Stripes are proof that two can make just as much noise as three or four.

The White Stripes are proof that two can make just as much noise as three or four

"The White Stripes was just the first time I'd latched onto a modern thing," says Jack. "It was an easy thing to do because me and Meg could just set up to play after work, just the two of us. I'd been in other bands... it never worked. With just a two-piece band, you can't have someone forming alliances..."

As members of the Y Generation, a case could be made that The White Stripes are atypically traditional. They tell us, in interviews, in influences and even in their choice to marry young that the old world *is* of interest to them. For goodnessakes, there is a picture of early 20th century songwriter Cole Porter in the *Elephant* booklet. Not many rock guys Jack's age (except for maybe Rufus Wainwright) have a perceptible interest in Porter and his fellow Tin Pan Alley writers like George Gershwin, Irving Berlin and Hoagy Carmichael. And yet from his Midwestern upbringing to his drive to pen top-quality songs, in standards-king Porter, Jack has found yet another role model from whom he can derive inspiration.

When it comes to gender roles, The White Stripes play it fairly straight – Jack more classically aggressive and dominant over Meg's demure and withdrawn public persona. And yet, Jack is good as a dramatic, preening frontman and rock's traditional "low man on the totem pole," and the drummer is a woman doing a job that not many of her sisters have chosen (we can count the major female drummers on one hand). Think of women drummers these days and Meg is the one whose name is called out. Like Ringo and Keith Moon, she balances her songwriter's weightiness with a lightness of spirit and innate ability to judge exactly what her band needs and when and where it needs it.

On *Elephant*'s cover, the two former sweethearts are sitting on... a trunk. They're dressed as old-time country singers. Meg is crying, her circulation cut off

Think of women drummers these days and Meg is the one whose name is called out

by a cord at the ankle and her feet blue – she would appear to be tied to this circus against her will (like a baby elephant attached to its mother?); Jack holds a cricket bat (the British version of a baseball bat) as he sits under the glare of a light bulb. The human skull by Meg belongs to Jack's personal collection. The sweetheart is dead. Like some freaky sideshow act (celebrity photographer Annie Lebovitz also shot them as a knife thrower and his trusty assistant) from another era, this rare breed of (inbred?) show people has come to entertain us.

I'm just happy to dig Jack and Meg for the aforementioned good humor and new grown-up sexiness, for the submersion of the child-like stuff (the baby talk has got to go – 'Little People,' good-bye) and the return to rock. It's been a long time since there was a hard-rock band to like that wasn't stupid, and The White Stripes is it; their minimalist and smart, crunchy rock is more powerful than the sound of the heaviest metal thunder. They literally could have gone in any direction they'd wanted after *White Blood Cells*, but on *Elephant*, lord have mercy, they let it rock.

Find a home

Nope, it's not a bass – the first notes we hear at the start of 'Seven Nation Army' – but what a great trick. It's Jack's guitar through an octave pedal. Geezers may be reminded of Cream's tune 'SWLABR.' And an old Bob Seger System garage classic from the home state just might be the source of the song's super-riff.

This interview extract is taken from a talk with Canada's Nardwuar The Human Serviette (!):

"Now tell me how cool Seger is. He is a cool guy isn't he, Meg?"

MEG: "He is awesome. The first album is amazing."

JACK: "Early Bob Seger System."

"A lot of people are dissing the Seger. But he's down with it isn't he?"

JACK: "They need to get back to the Bob Seger System. You have to find the Bob Seger System Band. '2+2 Is On My Mind' is my favorite song."

Apart from anything else it illustrates how, when The White Stripes are being asked proper questions about music, they are engaged rather than enraged. And yet they have been painted as the perpetually annoyed American

They've got a right to be mad, and they let it rip on 'Seven Nation Army'

gothic couple: they've got a right to be mad and they let it rip on *Elephant* opener 'Seven Nation Army.'

"That song's about gossip," says Jack. "'Seven Nation Army' is about this character who is involved in the realm of gossip with his friends and family and is so enraged by it that he wants to leave town. It's about me, Meg and the people we're dating. The world constantly tries to dissect people, chew them up and spit them out. We get that all the time…"

The search for home is now desperate – a necessity:

"I'm going to Wichita, far from this opera for evermore
I'm gonna work the straw
Make the sweat drip out of every pore
And I'm bleeding and I'm bleeding
And I'm bleeding
Right before the lord
All the words are gonna bleed from me and I will think
No more
And the stains coming from my blood
Tell me go back home
Tell me go back home"

'Seven Nation Army' (its title apparently inspired by Jack's childhood mispronunciation of Salvation Army) spent more than 37 weeks on *Billboard's* US Modern Rock Tracks chart in 2003; it peaked at Number One, where it stood for four weeks.

The next single to shock the airwaves was the nasty little 'The Hardest Button To Button,' which spent six weeks in the Top Ten at the end of 2003. Jack displays his subtle, shapeshifting vocal qualities during the song, a great piece of storytelling. Tough as nails on the verse, he's stoic and stiff, almost like a rapper; though by the time the baby starts crying and he gets hold of that rag doll, he's starting to come unglued (just like in 'Stop Breakin' Down,' that baby has got to stop). When it comes around to *"something else to show you,"* there's an edge – a downright scary quaver. Slowly, that next verse escalates – the opinions that don't matter, the brain like pancake batter, the stick, the dog, and the box with something in it... getting shakier... all building toward that trembling *"Uh-oh."* Brilliant.

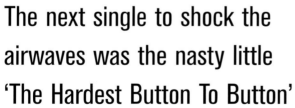

The next single to shock the airwaves was the nasty little 'The Hardest Button To Button'

The speedy 'Hypnotize' is vibrating old-school punk/garage revival while trashy blues-rock is the tone of the Yardbirdsy 'Girl You Have No Faith In Medicine,' (which by now fans seem to know is all about girls who don't like to take pills – Jack told *Mojo* that Meg had some problems with this song, and he took out some of the original lyrics).

The Burt Bacharach easy-rock serenade, 'I Just Don't Know What To Do With Myself' is a soul-punk power rocker when Jack sings it. The vocals are delivered with the kind of desperation that the Sixties pop idols (Dusty Springfield, Dionne Warwicke) who previously recorded it had never actually reached. The pair originally cut it at the BBC Maida Vale studio for Radio 1; it had been previously released as a CD single b-side to 'Fell In Love With A Girl.'

Jack wrote 'In The Cold Cold Night' especially for Meg to sing

Jack wrote 'In the Cold, Cold Night' especially for Meg to sing; it sounds like the Whites doing a tribute to the Peggy Lee cocktail classic 'Fever,' although Jack claims to have had Mazzy Star on his mind in addition to Lee. Both songs fill the 'show tune' quotient for the record.

'The Air Near My Fingers' is bound in the British Invasion-style pop that Jack puts into practice on each album; sweet vocalizing and one of those do-doot singalongs which have become a Stripey habit. 'You've Got Her In Your Pocket' is more of the vulnerable balladry at which he excels.

'Little Acorns' was an accident, says Jack: "It was a two-track [tape] of commercials that I was recording piano over. It was a radio commercial – a friend of mine duplicates radio commercials … it was on the reel. When I played it back, that story was on the other track. It seemed to go along with the music perfect. I finished writing the story about the squirrel." Be like the squirrel...

Critics really enjoyed their comparisons between 'There's No Home For You Here' and Queen's 'Bohemian Rhapsody;' a big fan of both songs, it wasn't the first thing that occurred to me, which is to say that we all get what we get from the White Stripes' version of Name That Tune – it's half the fun.

"I layered vocals over vocals… It's anti-anything we've ever done," Jack says. It's also one of the meanest songs in The White Stripes' catalog – its use of the word "stupid" right up there with Neil Young's hateful 'Stupid Girl' and the Rolling Stones' song of the same title/different tune.

By the end of 2003, *Elephant* had sold over three million copies worldwide. It looked like it was about to sweep top honors in the critic's polls too. The White Stripes were nominated for Grammy Awards in four categories: Album Of The Year, Best Alternative Album, Best Rock Performance By A Duo Or Group With Vocal ('Seven Nation Army') and Best Rock Song ('Seven Nation Army'). The band continued to tour, and would do so presumably until they no longer could. All work and no play… you know the rest.

"Sometimes I get jealous of people who can enjoy it," says Jack on the topic of success. "Freddie Mercury could do both. He was amazing for that. He loved the monstrosity of being a rock star."

You know, I just don't think of Queen when I think of The White Stripes, but maybe I should start considering it. Then again, by the time Jack made that comment, he might not have been thinking very clearly (Mercury might've enjoyed it all right, but after all, he's no longer with us). Were The White Stripes suffering from road burn and possible media over-saturation? Maybe they figured you only go around once or twice so, like Freddie Mercury, you may as well have a good time. They were definitely having their fun the best way they knew how.

Meg had cracked her wrist in February and did all the pre-press for the album in her cast, though she was ready to hit the road in April upon the album's release.

Were The White Stripes suffering from road burn and media over-saturation?

Elephant came out on April Fool's Day 2003, and the band had a few tricks up their sleeves. The Whites had elected not to do the usual pre-release advance CDs normally reserved for the media and retailers, for fear of internet bootlegging by excitable children. But they decided to press vinyl advances, and leak them especially early, specifically to foil journalists who didn't own turntables.

When the band appeared on *Conan O'Brien* for an unprecedented-on-late-night-television four nights running, a massive African-American man dressed in gangster gear which matched Jack's stood near Meg during and after her performance. So who was he...?

"He was an LA cop," says Jack, "a bronze medallist in Greco-Roman wrestling at the Pan Am games and a percussionist for Rick James. We had to hire him." Funny enough. But when Jack beckoned for him to fetch some furniture polish to clean off O'Brien's desk... well, is that funny?

I consider everything other than the music to be a trick

"I consider everything other than the music to be a trick," says Jack. "How you present yourself, how the album is packaged, how the production of a song is. It's all tricks. The only thing that's truth is the story. Everything around it – all the way up to magazine photos – is a trick ... The goal is to share with people, but if we can trick 15-year-old girls into singing the lyrics to a Son House song, we've really achieved something."

The White Stripes were on a roll. But how long were they going to be able to maintain life in the three-ring circus?

Chapter 6

21st century
blues

"'Tell me Boll Weevil,
what make yo' head so red?'
'Been workin' on yo' cotton,
Till I'm almost dead'"

'THE BOLL WEEVIL HOLLER,'
ADAPTED BY JOHN & ALAN LOMAX

above: Son House (1902-1988)
right: Meg at the Masonic Temple, 2003

The **White Stripes**

itting the road after the release of *Elephant* in April 2003, touring was top priority for The White Stripes for the rest of the year. More people than ever were about to witness The White Stripes live on stage: the place where the power of the two's music is made manifest. Contrary to the way they look in most photographs – the Mr and Ms goth rock, the coy children, the annoyed adults, the stylish mannequins – the Whites do not pose on-stage. Jack provides the melody, Meg provides the rhythm and the story is told by the songs throughout the show.

The White Stripes never plan what they're going to play, though there may be certain combinations of songs that work best night after night.

"We put a lot of pressure on ourselves live. We don't have a set list, we don't rehearse and we don't play the tunes exactly like on the album," says Jack. The three restrictions combined ensure that at each unique White Stripes gig there is a palpable, anything-can-happen energy in the air. It is that magical intangible which The White Stripes brought back to rock'n'roll. You can't put a price on it, and it's what books like this take pages explaining: spontaneity is rock'n'roll's essence, and its absence is what left people proclaiming it dead.

Before they take the stage, a reel of vintage cartoons plays – among them those starring America's animated sweetheart of the 1930s, Betty Boop. In the Boop cartoon *Snow White*, bandleader Cab Calloway performs 'St James Infirmary,' which reminds us not only of The White Stripes' first album, but of the pantheon of 20th century masters on which they consistently rely for inspiration, from *Citizen Kane* to Bob Dylan. The cartoons may also be the signal that you are in for an evening's entertainment of the good, old-fashioned variety. The set-up also had me thinking whether The White Stripes had constructed their evenings like a traditional minstrel show, in three parts: the first third devoted to songs of all types, the second third the novelty songs, and finally the songs that tell a story… Nah, couldn't be.

They almost always play 'Death Letter' – a real showpiece where anything is liable to happen; it's Meg who seems to lead Jack on this one through its sidewinder-ish tempos. It's the one where Jack might meet her back-to-back on the drum stool or even stand on a piece of the kit or drop to his knees. Sometimes they'll turn it into a Son House medley: 'Death Letter'/'Grinnin' In Your Face'/'John The Revelator.' Jack shouts directions at Meg, she speeds, she slows, it's fast, it's not, it's outta control. It's folk music, it's goth-rock and it's deep blues, all rolled into one.

Other nights they might skip the song you came to hear (they've left out 'Fell In Love With A Girl' on more than one occasion).

The big US summer tours that year – *Lollapalooza*, *Ozzfest* and Metallica's *Summer Sanitarium* – were exciting enough, though it was the upcoming White Stripes' shows that were creating the loudest anticipatory noise. The venues were bigger, some of the largest The White Stripes had yet to headline in the US. The same was true in the UK and Ireland where they'd earned top summer billing at *T In The Park* near Edinburgh, the hard rock-dominated Leeds and Reading festivals and Dublin's *Witness*. From there, it was the world: Japan, Australia, South America. But wherever The White Stripes perform – at the Gold Dollar in 1997 or Glastonbury in 2002, in front of ten or 10,000 – they insist on putting on a show. They are born entertainers. Among their many rules: the show must go on, no matter what (unless perhaps someone breaks a hand, of course...) And you always know if it's been a good show for them if they come back for a finale encore of 'Boll Weevil'

Spontaneity is rock'n'roll's essence, and its absence is what left people proclaiming it dead

(also known as the 'Boll Weevil Song,' 'The Boll Weevil Holler' and 'Bo Weevil Blues.')

As Meg explains, "If we don't really feel any energy coming from the crowd, we don't usually play it…"

Like any number of songs in the folk, blues and English ballad tradition, 'Boll Weevil' is based on a real-life event turned into folk story turned into song. In African-American folk tale tradition, real people – the ruthless 'Staggolee,' railroader 'Casey Jones,' tough gal 'Frankie,' strongman 'John Henry,' and trickster 'Long Gone John' – were the inspiration behind some of today's best-known traditional songs. And so it was with the tiny, black 'Boll Weevil' – the story derives from a plague of insects that spread from Mexico to Texas and moved throughout the South, devastating its cotton crops in the late 19th century. Naturally, white land-owners wanted to see the boll weevil problem controlled and eradicated; African-Americans found something to identify with in the insect's plight: he's lookin' for a home.

The song's evolution as a classic began when the earliest of blues singers, Ma Rainey, made 'Bo-weavil [sic] Blues' her signature tune in her live show; she recorded it for Paramount in the 1920s. Charley Patton, as the Masked Marvel, called his 1929 version 'Mississippi Boweavil Blues,' and Blind Willie McTell had his 'Boll Weavil' in 1940. All versions set in motion the song's evolution as a classic. The version by Leadbelly, included on his *Library Of Congress Recordings* is perhaps best known, though the rock and soul versions by Eddie Cochran and Brooke Benton respectively are remembered by rock fans of a certain age.

When we came along they wanted to chew us up and spit us out

As the band's international profile continued to swell – thanks to word-of-mouth and reviews on the electrifying gigs, as well as radio and video airplay and television appearances – the newsstand magazine articles multiplied, breeding White Stripes cover stories. It seemed that *any man with a microphone* was granted his interview with Jack and Meg: literary journals, lifestyle digests, webzines, even the most tasteless American rawk magazine, all did their best to reveal a little bit of the real White Stripes.

"That's all the media wants to do," says Jack. "They want to dissect everything. When we came along they wanted to chew us up and spit us out. It was like, 'Let's get the *real* story. Let's learn everything about them and in three months from now we'll never have to hear about them again.'"

And yet, for all of the interviews they've granted, The White Stripes have managed to reveal very little about themselves and the origins of their music. For a pair who extol the virtue of truth, there is so much that remains unknown about Jack and especially Meg White. The colors, the numbers, the costumes, the parables and all the other tricks have provided a great wall of protection for the two, who appear to take privacy and mystery as values commeasurable with the truth. Their persistent shifting of focus away from themselves and onto the things that inspire them – whether it's Betty Boop, Bob Dylan or their own hometown's cache of unheralded dirt-rock meisters from The Gories to the Soledad Brothers – is in the great tradition of torchbearers and storytellers who came before them.

Like the bluesmen and women of yore, The White Stripes' habit of borrowing and carrying on song traditions is one of the things that bolsters their strength. The critic's old saw, "the shock of recognition," applies to the songs of Jack White, with their often repeated words, themes and evocation of the bygone world. Just as a group of visionaries in 1950s Memphis borrowed from hillbilly and blues music to come up with rock'n'roll, in early 21st century Detroit The White Stripes borrow from blues, rock and this-and-that to make something new too. Add

The White Stripes have always managed to reveal very little about themselves and their music

to that the fact that they speak to children, adults and hard-to-please critics – and they did it all in the space of a few short years – and you've got a case for a new kind of 21st century blues.

In July of 2003, after marching forward for 19 weeks, 'Seven Nation Army' took over the Number One spot on *Billboard's* Modern Rock Tracks chart by nudging out the lame 'Send The Pain Below' by Chevelle (a hard-rock trio of actual brothers from Chicago). The White Stripes now shared the Top Ten spotlight with the crème de la US hard-rock acts – the reformed Jane's Addiction, Seattle's Foo Fighters, and the supergroups Audio Slave and Queens Of The Stone Age – all of whom heavily feature members on the wrong side of 30. Here was yet more evidence (as if any was needed) that newer bands continued to wage back-to-basics war on the synthetic sound of alternative rock radio. No, this was not a media and marketing trick – this was new garage rock in a full-court press, moving over the old guard. *Elephant* would go on to sell in the millions, just as *White Blood Cells* had done.

By mid-summer 2003, the band had been nominated in four categories in the *MTV Video Music Awards*, where last time they'd struck gold. This year the clip of choice was 'Seven Nation Army' with its simple, retro video effects and some Ray Harryhausen-style stop-action animation (those skeletons are a little like the seven swordfighters in *Jason & The Argonauts*). The band made more videos with Michel Gondry for the 'The Hardest Button To Button' and 'Black Math.'

The former, starring multiple drum kits, guitars and amps, caused Jack to proclaim, "It's the greatest video we've ever made. I think it's one of the greatest videos ever made. I can't stop watching it. I've watched it 50 times, probably."

Jack and Meg had already made it through the first leg of the US tour and returned home for an all-American red, white and blues 4th of July. It was right in time for Jack to put in an appearance at the opening of Dave Buick and Dion Fischer's record store, Young Soul Rebels, adjacent to the Magic Stick on Woodward Avenue in downtown Detroit – the nexus of the Detroit garage scene (along with the Lager House) since the closing of the Gold Dollar. This was followed by his own 28th birthday celebration on July 9th. He'd even brought his new girlfriend, the actress Renee Zellweger, home for the occasion.

The big question on everyone's mind was, 'Will Jack play the guitar again?'

But the next day, the unsettling news came over the wire services: Jack and Renee had been in an auto accident – he'd injured his hand, she was fine. Follow-up reports specified that it was a compound fracture to his left index finger. Fans around the world sat out the weekend in anticipation of more news, but the big question on everyone's mind obviously was, 'Will Jack play the guitar again?'

It took a couple of days but when word finally came through, The White Stripes' summer tour was off. Six weeks of dates booked for July and August were postponed, just three days after *Elephant* had hit that top spot on the US charts.

"The White Stripes deeply value the relationship they have with their fans and regret any inconvenience caused by these current events and are thankful for their patience and understanding," the duo said in a statement.

As the week closed out, more information was made available about the crash, but no one had actually heard from the Stripes themselves, or about the real disposition of Jack's hand. Eight days after the accident, he left these words on the website:

"Hello candy cane children,
I broke my finger, three breaks, car wreck, horrible left turn in front of me, no chance of escape, air bag, the air near my fingers, devil in my left hand, doctors say no way, lots of pain, typing with one finger, made it through year of rock'n'roll death, got off with just a warning.

"Apologies to those wishing to see my hand live, soon enough I'm sure, now me and meg can share war stories, I love when we share, like once there was a monkey, and we shared the experience as children do." – JACK WHITE III

With the rest of the summer to recover, the Whites stayed busy. Jack posted a video clip of his hand surgery on the band's official website to quell rumors that his accident may have been faked to avoid touring. The gesture seemed a bit unnecessary but, he says, "I always watch surgery documentaries on TV, and I just thought it was an interesting little film on its own." Doctors inserted three screws in his hand.

In the meantime, talk around town was that Meg had bought one of those *Fall Of The House Of Usher* mansions in downtown Detroit's Brush Park, and Jack one of his own in nearby Indian Village; he was also photographed by paparazzi, dining in New York and Los Angeles, with Zellweger and Beck. Meg took to the road with her friends in the Soledad Brothers.

In August they were conspicuously absent from the *MTV Music Awards* (though an official fan website, Triple Tremelo, posted a picture of Meg and a girlfriend smiling for cameras on the red carpet). Meg also jetted over to London for the *Carling Weekend* to hang with friends at the festivals. There was also time to film the pair's segment of Jim Jarmusch's *Coffee & Cigarettes*, which also features Iggy Pop, Tom Waits, indie film actors Alfred Molina and Steve Buscemi and comedian Steve Coogan. And Jack also began production on the Loretta Lynn album.

"She wanted to make one final album … I put my name in, and they let me have a chance at it. It worked out really well. Me and Loretta have become pretty good friends since last year, and I think we work together really well," he says.

"There's some kind of connection with us. I feel really comfortable with her, and I think she feels really comfortable with me, which I'm really glad for, because I could see someone like me – the way I look or whatever – not being appealing, or her thinking that maybe I wasn't down with the kind of music she does. She could tell that we had the same love for the same things about music."

It appears that every moment Jack isn't on-stage or in the studio with Meg, he's in the studio with someone else. He claims it's not him on his pals the Electric Six's 'Danger! High Voltage' (it tore up the UK, didn't do so hot in the States); he also played parts for DJ Mark Ronson, but the project was scrapped.

In the summer of *Elephant*, the rock world was hungry for White Stripes news – and any news would do

You have to wonder if any of the above tangential White Stripes activity would have even made the radar had they been able to remain on tour, but in the summer of *Elephant*, the rock world was hungry for White Stripes news – and any news would do.

Back in Detroit, Jack went to see the reformed Iggy & The Stooges play the show postponed from the week before. But the mood shifted as the week unfolded. The band's latest video to accompany the September 1st release of the UK single of 'I Just Don't Know What To Do With Myself' created a controversy before it was even aired: model Kate Moss appears in it, pole-dancing like a stripper. The video's director was filmmaker Sofia Coppola (coincidentally or not, her first film was an adaptation of a book based in the Detroit-area, *The Virgin Suicides* by Detroit writer Jeffrey Eugenides). Coppola comes with a super-high pedigree in the fashion and film industries – though that did not necessarily make her the best person to direct a White Stripes video.

Jack said, "I don't have much to say about it. It was completely Sofia Coppola's idea and I don't really have a comment on it."

The *New York Times Magazine* reported that at the video shoot Jack had muttered, "We'll get Meg up on the pole after lunch."

Laura Barton of the UK's *Guardian* newspaper *did* have a comment on the video that week: the headline of her editorial read, "Stripping isn't cool: public debasement of women is never trendy, no matter what the celebs say."

And me, well, I handed in my invisible White Stripes Fan Club Membership ID for about 24 hours.

Was it a trick, or a misstep? I guess, like the songs, we all have our own version of what it means and so, until Jack decides to add anything, we'll never know. I've decided to block out the whole incident, as if I had never heard or read any of it – what can we do? The Rolling Stones, to mention but one offending rock band, are not lilywhite in this department either.

By mid-week, August 27th, Jack had issued a *Pilgrim's Progress*-like allegory via the website, underscoring the band's developing philosophy around the idea of the Truth. Parables and allegories are devices that Dylan, as we've seen, has also used to fuel the mystique, and The White Stripes – through the use of Biblical language and red, white and three clues – are happy to spice up their own myth on a semi-regular basis as well.

Here's a portion of what Jack wrote this time:

"Hello little children
There was a possibility, and it was retriever who discovered this, his wits got keen earlier and now he knows this and tells me to tell you…When two or three are gathered in my name I am there with them, when two or three are gathered socially there becomes a new air in the room…three people are sitting on a bench, one of them, let's call her "amazing" says to one of the others, let's call him "Mr Cotton," don't you think that the sun burns beautifully? And Mr Cotton replies (truthfully this time), "Well amazing, is it not my right to deny the beauty of the sun, even when it shines in my face? Must I always agree with you for you are my mother?… But the third person had something interesting to say. Her name was exemplify, and she was not happy at the state of the union. She quietly spoke, don't you both know that there are three truths? …one truth is

what your own perception is, the other truth is what the collective perception is, and the third truth is THE truth, the only one that cannot bend and is constant for as long as the object, feeling, emotion, or instance lasts, this is the truth that only god knows, and that we only pretend to comprehend..."
– JACK WHITE III

Who is 'I' and who is 'she?' Is Mr Cotton a reference to the lead in *The Third Man*, actor Joseph Cotton, or is it the South's beloved King Cotton? Mercifully, there would be no more reason or time to ponder the minutiae of The White Stripes' non-musical activity: the moment for them to return to the stage had finally arrived.

On September 13th, still unable to make the movements necessary to form a C chord, Jack was nonetheless ready to give his finger a shot at the fretboard in front of an audience. The pair had spent the day prior to the gig rehearsing at the

Jack reverently rambled through a spoken-word tribute to Johnny Cash, who had passed away that week

Warfield Theater in San Francisco, site of previous live triumphs. The following night, in front of a sold-out crowd of eight thousand, the two bounded on-stage at the Greek Theater, Berkeley. Meg hopped into place on her candy-striped stool; Jack grabbed a guitar and promptly broke a string as they lit into 'The Big Three Killed My Baby.'

Death was on the dance-card as they chomped through 'Dead Leaves And The Dirty Ground' and followed with 'When I Hear My Name.' Jack reverently rambled through a spoken-word tribute to Johnny Cash, who had passed away that week. They reclaimed their ground during a killer 'Death Letter,' complete with an a cappella jam of 'Grinnin' In Your Face.' 'Black Math,' 'Apple Blossom,' 'You're Pretty Good Looking' – all pitch perfect – then they slid into the sex-charged numbers: Meg's 'In The Cold Cold Night' and Jack's 'I Just Don't Know What To Do With Myself.' The young girls in the crowd swayed, swooned and sung along word-for-word to both. The blues were represented during 'Cannon'/'John The Revelator' (it was turning into Son House night), 'Ball And Biscuit' and 'Hardest Button To Button,' which seemed to catch the attention of the guitar fans and rockers in the house. Pause to refresh with 'We're Going To Be Friends' and closing out with a medley of 'Isis'/'Let's Shake Hands'/'Man' by the Yeah Yeah Yeahs/'Pick A Bale Of Cotton' by Leadbelly, and then whoosh, they abandoned the stage.

The gig was a triumph, because Jack made it through. The White Stripes were back

It was hard to say what to make of it, but when they encored with 'Seven Nation Army,' 'Little Room,' 'Union Forever,' 'Truth Doesn't Make A Noise,' and the traditional singalong 'Boll Weevil,' it became clear the gig was a triumph, because Jack made it through. The White Stripes were back.

Ten days after Berkeley, and after a week back on the road, Jack's finger was working just right for the band's three sold-out LA shows. The White Stripes turned in a performance at the Greek Theatre that will go down as one of the greats on the *Elephant* tour. The Soledad Brothers opened with their manic-blues; The Yeah Yeah Yeahs followed. When The White Stripes entered, they cut to the chase with the searing electro-shock of 'Black Math' and some hard-pounding versions of 'Dead Leaves And The Dirty Ground' and 'Hotel Yorba.' So frantic were 'When I Hear My Name' and 'Cannon,' Jack's keyboard set-up barreled to the floor. Barefoot Meg is becoming so confident center-stage singing 'In The Cold Cold Night' that she's even starting to camp it up a bit. The unstoppable 'Hardest Button To Button' had Jack busting out in that tip-toe version of the moonwalk he does. 'Astro,' with Screaming Lord Sutch's 'Jack The Ripper' slashed through with Buddy Holly's 'Words Of Love' and 'I Can Only Give You Everything' by Them (or was it 'Devil's Haircut' by Beck?) slid into 'Look Me Over Closely,' and was followed by a frantic 'Lafayette Blues'/'Ready Teddy' – sung in French. The people in the pit were with them 100 per cent, while the rest of the house looked dumbstruck.

They farewelled on this night with 'Let's Build A Home'/'Goin' Back To

Memphis.' And as they delivered those final verses it seemed clear that The White Stripes have at least found a temporary home on-stage. In front of thousands, playing their songs – that's where Jack and Meg live and breathe, it's where they are nourished and find shelter from the storm. The velocity of the set that night was astonishing. But it was the subdued 'Do' from the first album that was the showstopper – and positively poignant on this starry Southern California night. Having shared stages with The Rolling Stones, Jeff Beck, Iggy Pop, Loretta Lynn and plenty more, these days the song takes on a whole different meaning.

"And then my idols walk next to me / I look up at them they fade away
It's a destruction of a mystery / The more I listen to what they say"

"When your idols are telling you that they love what you're doing – like Bob Dylan sent down word that he's a fan – what do you do with *that*?" says Jack. "It's really hard to understand what you should think about that sort of thing."

Like their idols, from the bluesmen of the Mississippi Delta to Dylan and Loretta Lynn, it is quite possible that The White Stripes are forging a career with a potential for similar longevity. Will they choose, like Lynn, to immortalize themselves, writing their own history before it's over and further embedding their hopeful, self-stylized myth into a story for future generations? Or like Dylan, will they continue to live inside the protection of the myth of their own making and withhold comment till it's nearly all over?

We may think we know the stories of the key bluesmen in The White Stripes' story – Son House, Blind Willie McTell, Blind Willie Johnson and Robert Johnson – but do we really? Their myths and legends grow larger with the passing of the years. And yet The White Stripes seem to have an extraordinary connection to them: that place, those times, the people. Who could've predicted that this 21st century Northern man and woman would become sweethearts of the early 20th century's strictly Southern, country blues?

Bob Dylan sent down word that he's a fan – what do you do with *that*?

Somewhere along the way, Jack picked up on the idea that the closer we get to the root, the closer we are to its liberating qualities. He felt it when he heard Son House's 'Grinnin' In Your Face' for the first time. Like he said, it freed his life. When Jack returned to the root, rock'n'roll was on its way home.

> The closer we are to the root, the closer we are to its liberating qualities

The White Stripes show that with proper care and feeding, popular music's prodigal child, rock'n'roll, can thrive in the new millennium. As long as its roots are not forgotten, it will grow. With their music, The White Stripes have issued a handbook to the 20th century's panorama of sound: minstrelsy, Tin Pan Alley, blues, hillbilly, primitive rock'n'roll. At the time they were called on to re-inject Detroit Rock City with some soulful rock'n'blues magic, rock music and the city itself seemed irredeemable. And yet The White Stripes are a demonstration that, when there is hope, even things that appear dead can spring back to life, phoenix-like.

Sometimes in order to break the rules, you have to make some rules. But as long as there is a Mississippi of the mind, as long as there is a Delta, as long as there is an earth with its red and white hot core, as long as there are singers to sing, guitars to play and drums to beat, dreams to build and homes to find, there will be blues. And The White Stripes, in their powerful Detroit Rock way, have ensured that the people will be singing 'John The Revelator,' one more time.

Epilogue
Home sweet home

It was the biggest blackout in US history and the joke going around was that it was Iggy Pop's fault. On August 14th 2003 Iggy & The Stooges were scheduled to perform in Detroit for the first time in nearly 30 years. Detroit rock's finest were in the house at the DTE Energy Music Theatre, a few miles from town – The Von Bondies got the support slot. Iggy & The Stooges (original members Ron and Scott Ashton with former Minuteman Mike Watt filling in for Dave Alexander on bass) had been soundchecking when at just about 4pm Eastern Standard Time, the states of New York, Ohio, parts of Canada and all of Michigan lost all electrical power. Detroit would be dark that night – power was not completely restored throughout Michigan for almost 48 hours and there was a boil-water order in effect throughout the state. I landed at Detroit's Wayne County Airport at about 4:05 that day and spent the next 36 hours in the dark with the rest of Michigan's 2.1 million energy consumers.

One hundred thousand autoworkers were given the day off on Friday as Ford and General Motors closed their assembly plants. But reports of Detroit's state of emergency were grossly exaggerated in the national media. Only the usual number of arrests (118) were made on the first night of the blackout, and the 11pm curfew for minors – in effect every night of the year – yielded only 15 juvenile arrests. It was a quiet night in Detroit City.

"Before you pick up a brick and throw it, before you tip over a car, before you take a TV, you better ask yourself, is this worth ten years of my life?" warned Wayne County prosecutor Michael Duggan on day two of the blackout. Thirty-four-year-old mayor Kwame M. Kilpatrick came on a little softer: "The party has to happen in your homes tonight," he declared at a news conference called 24 hours after the lights went out. "Continue your family time. Love they neighbor – in your own home, your own neighborhood." And so residents waited in line for gas at the few stations that were open and queued for water for the most part without incident. This was a long way from the Detroit riots of 1967, that devastating event which left the city shell-shocked for decades. Detroit's setbacks are the perfect set-up for a comeback. Throughout the crisis the mayor proudly referred to the "New Detroit" and "The renaissance we've created."

That same weekend, Jason Stollsteimer of The Von Bondies shared wedding vows with Andrea Wehenkel as scheduled, and the Detroit rock family turned out again for the occasion. At the rockin' wedding reception that followed, Jeff Stollsteimer's soul revue, The Elevations, got things fired things up as friends and relatives hit the dancefloor. Dave Buick and Dion Fischer spun garage rock and Eighties new wave sides. Brendan Benson and the groom with his Von Bondies closed out the big day with freewheeling abandon. The Cobras, Paybacks and a Bantam Rooster stalked the halls of the mysterious and the many-storied Masonic Temple – where, coincidentally, The White Stripes would be headlining in a few more weeks. But on this night, The White Stripes were nowhere to be found. Jack was in Los Angeles; I never did hear how Meg spent the weekend of the biggest blackout in US history.

I hope that someday we find out that Jack and Meg really are brother and sister. Alternatively, I hope it's true that they love one another, and that Jack is Meg's right-hand man until her tiny hands grow old. Maybe the truth is not in the opposites – maybe everything is just as it seems, just as it's meant to be. Jack and Meg, two young and creative people with a deep soul connection, formed a rock band. It was successful. And when enough was enough, they had the good sense to figure it out for themselves and be done with it.

Meg's vision of The White Stripes' future is clear: "In ten years, for us still to be up on-stage, still singing stuff wearing red and white, it's not going to be relevant," she says. "We'll know exactly when that's over – when we're repeating ourselves or when it's just not there anymore. We'll know."

A brief
concordance

Some important White Stripes words, and the songs in which they appear:

APPLE

'Apple Blossom' – *Hey little apple blossom*

'Screwdriver' – *What if someone walked up to me and like an apple cut right through me*

BABY (sweetheart)

'The Big Three Killed My Baby' – *The big three killed my baby… and I think that my baby is dead*

'Hypnotize' – *I want to hypnotize you baby on the telephone*

'I'm Finding It Harder To Be A Gentleman' – *I feel comfortable so baby why don't you feel the same*

'Let's Build A Home' – *Some bricks now baby let's build a home*

'Let's Shake Hands' – *Baby let's shake hands… Baby let's be friends…* and *Baby say my name*

'Lord Send Me An Angel' (Blind Willie McTell) – *Where did my baby go, McTell?*

'Stop Breakin' Down' (Robert Johnson) – *I give my baby now the 90 degree*

'St James Infirmary' (traditional) – *See my baby there*

'Your Southern Can Is Mine' (Blind Willie McTell) – *You might take it from the south baby hide it up north*

BABY (infant)

'The Hardest Button to Button' – *It was a baby boy, so we bought him a toy …* and *We named him 'Baby'*

'Sugar Never Tasted So Good' – *I felt just like a baby, until I held a baby*

BED

'Jimmy The Exploder' – *Yeah monkey, jumping on the bed now*

'Little People' – *There's a little girl with a tiger on her bed*

'We're Going To Be Friends' – *Tonight I'll dream while I'm in bed*

BIRD

'Hello Operator' – *Find a canary, a bird to bring my message home*

'Little Bird' – *I got a little bird, I'm gonna take her home*

BLEEDING/BLOOD

'The Big Three Killed My Baby' – *The motor's runnin' on trucker's blood*

'Seven Nation Army' – *And the stains coming from my blood…* and *I'm bleeding and I'm bleeding and I'm bleeding right before the lord*

BONE/BONES

'Let's Build A Home' – *I'm getting lazy won't you throw me a bone*

'St James Infirmary' (traditional) – *Take apart your bones and put 'em back together*

'Screwdriver' – *Whenever you go out alone, take a little dog a bone*

'Seven Nation Army' – *And the feeling coming from my bones says find a home*

'Truth Doesn't Make A Noise' – *And the quiver of her bones below*

BRAIN

'Black Math' – *Is it the fingers or the brain that you're teaching a lesson*

'Fell In Love With A Girl' – *These two sides of my brain need to have a meeting…* and *My left brain knows that all love is fleeting*

'Lovesick' (Bob Dylan) – *And my brain is so wired*

'Seven Nation Army' – *I had a brain that felt like pancake batter*

'Sugar Never Tasted So Good' – *If the wrinkle that is in your brain*

'Stop Breakin' Down' (R. Johnson) – *The stuff I got'll bust your brains out*

BRICKS

'Broken Bricks' – *Been to the broken bricks girl*

'Let's Build A Home' – *Some bricks now baby let's build a home*

'Your Southern Can Is Mine' (McTell) – *I'm gettin' me a brick outta my backyard… and I'm gonna grab me a brick and tear your can on down*

BUS

'I'm Bound To Pack It Up' – *The bus is warm and softly lit*

'Sister Do You Know My Name?' – *And the bus is pulling up to your house*

CIGARETTES

'A Boy's Best Friend' – *A pack of dogs and cigarettes*

'Seven Nation Army' – *Behind a cigarette*

CRANE

'Sugar Never Tasted So Good' – *Your fingers have become a crane*

'Broken Bricks' – *Climb the metal of a broken crane*

DECEMBER

'The Air Near My Fingers' – *You told me in December*

'The Same Boy You've Always Known' – *Pretty tough to think about the beginning of December*

DOG/DOGS

'A Boy's Best Friend' – *My dogs come sit next to me, a pack of dogs and cigarettes*

'China Pig' (Captain Beefheart) – *I used to have a dog with me*

'Screwdriver' – *Whenever you go out alone, take a little dog a bone*

EASTER

'John The Revelator' (Blind Willie Johnson) – *One Easter morning…*

'I Fought Piranhas' – *Well it's Easter morning now*

FINGERS

'The Air Near My Fingers' (*title*)

'Black Math' – *My fingers definitely turning to black now* and *Is it the fingers or the brain that you're teaching a lesson*

'Expecting' – *But your fingers have shown me that your head is so clever*

'Let's Shake Hands' – *Put your fingers in my hand*

'Red Death At 6:14' – *With her fingers turning blue and her face turning red*

'Sugar Never Tasted So Good' – *Your fingers have become a crane*

FRIEND/FRIENDS

'Ball And Biscuit' – *Ask your girlfriends and see if they know*

'A Boy's Best Friend' – *My only friends speak no words to me*

'Let's Shake Hands' – *Baby, let's be friends*

'Offend In Every Way' – *And listen to these facts that everyone is my friend*

'Well It's True That We Love One Another' – *Maybe we should just be friends*

'We're Going To Be Friends' – *I can tell that we are gonna be friends*

HAND/HANDS

'The Big Three Killed My Baby' – *No money in my hand again…* and *My stickshift and my hands are swollen…* and *Now my hands are turnin' red*

'Black Math' – *Drawing a square with a pencil in hand*

'Expecting' – *I came back with handfuls*

'Girl, You Have No Faith In Medicine' – *And just hand it this way*

'Hand Springs' – *But right next to that was a boy I knew with a spring in his hand*

'Hypnotize' – *I want to hold your little hand if I can be so bold / And be your right hand man until your hands get old*

'Let's Shake Hands' – *Baby, let's shake hands…* and *Put your fingers in my hand*

'Little Acorns' – *The problems in hand are lighter than at heart*

'Lord Send Me An Angel' (McTell) – *I went down to the station, suitcase in my hand…* and *She ain't no hand-me-down*

'Same Boy You've Always Known' – *I hope you know a strong man who can lend you a hand lowering my casket*

165

'There's No Home For You Here' – *Hands moving upward propel the situation*

'Truth Doesn't Make A Noise' – *The motion of her tiny hand*

'Your Southern Can Is Mine' (McTell) – *When I hit you mama then you feel my hand*

'You've Got Her In Your Pocket' – *You search in your hand for something clever to say*

HAIR/CURL

'Fell In Love With A Girl' – *Red hair with a curl*

'Little Acorn' – *Straighten your curls…* and *Well your problems hide in your curls*

'Dead Leaves And The Dirty Ground' – *Soft hair and a velvet tongue*

HOME/HOUSE

'Ashtray Heart' (Captain Beefheart) – *Send your mother home your navel*

'The Big Three Killed My Baby' – *Nobody's coming home again*

'Boll Weevil' (traditional) – *These boll weevils are lookin' for a home*

'A Boy's Best Friend' – *Their home has run out of space*

'Dead Leaves And The Dirty Ground' – *Thirty notes in the mailbox will tell you that I'm coming home…* and *Then I come home / no one to wrap my arms around*

'The Hardest Button To Button' – *We started living in an old house*

'Hello Operator' – *Find a canary, a bird to send my message home…* and *Send papers to an empty home*

'Hotel Yorba' – *They got a dirty little road leading up to the house…* and *Sitting on the front porch of that home*

'Hypnotize' – *And though I knew you weren't home…* and *So many times I called your house just to hear the tone*

'I Can Learn' – *Drive you home, then wait by the phone*

'I Can't Wait' – *I wish this house felt like a home*

'Jumble, Jumble' – *All at my house, c'mon over*

'Let's Build A Home' – *Some bricks now baby let's build a home*

'Little Bird' – *I got a little bird I'm gonna take her home…* and *When I get you home this is how it goes*

'Screwdriver' – *Then you got to drive it home*

'Seven Nation Army' – *And the feeling coming from my bones says find a home…* and *The stains coming from my blood tell me go back home*

'Sister Do You Know My Name' – *And the bus is pulling up to your house*

'There's No Home For You Here' – *There's no home for you here girl go away*

'You've Got Her In Your Pocket' – *'Cause it's home sweet home*

MONEY

'The Big Three Killed My Baby' – *No money in my hand again*

'Hello Operator' – *How you gonna get the money?*

'Why Can't You Be Nicer To Me' – *I don't have any money*

'Your Southern Can Is Mine'(McTell) – *Some hot shot's got money gonna pull my bail*

MOTHER/MAMA

'The Air Near My Fingers' – *My mom is so caring*

'Ashtray Heart' (Captain Beefheart) – *Send your mother home your navel*

'Astro' – *Maybe Mama does the Astro*

'Ball And Biscuit' – *It was my mother who made me the seventh son*

'A Boy's Best Friend' – *A boy's best friend is his mother, or whatever has become his pet*

'Do' – *Then my mother tried to pick me up*

'I Want To Be the Boy To Warm Your Mother's Heart' – *I want to be the boy to warm your mother's heart…* and *While my mother baked a cake for you*

'One More Cup Of Coffee' (Dylan) – *Your sister sees the future like your mama and yourself*

'Screwdriver' – *I love people like a brother but I'm not gonna be their mother now*

NAME

'Candy Cane Children' – *Don't you know your name girl / boy*

'Girl, You Have No Faith In Medicine' – *Is it just the name upon the bottle…* and *To a well familiar name*

'The Hardest Button To Button' – *We named him 'Baby'*

'Jolene' (Dolly Parton) – *Cryin' when he calls your name*

'Let's Shake Hands' – *Baby say my name*

'Same Boy You've Always Known' – *Forgot my name of course*

'Sister Do You Know My Name' – *Sister, do you know my name*

'Suzy Lee' – *On it was my name*

'The Union Forever' – *You're not alive if you don't know his name*

'When I Hear My Name' – *When I hear my name I wanna disappear*

RED

'The Big Three Killed My Baby' – *Now my hands are turnin' red*

'China Pig' (Captain Beefheart) – *With a little red box*

'Fell In Love With A Girl' – *Red hair with a curl*

'Hand Springs' – *I took my girl to go bowling downtown at the red door…* and *I dropped my red bowling ball*

'Jimmy The Exploder' – *Now you seein' red now*

'Party Of Special Things To Do' (Captain Beefheart) – *The red queen*

'Red Bowling Ball Ruth' – *Red bowling ball, red bowling ball Ruth*

'Red Death At 6:14' – *And her face was turning red*

'Boll Weevil' (traditional) – *What makes yo' face so red*

ROOM

'A Boy's Best Friend' – *Empty rooms and a telephone*

'Little Room' – *When you're in your little room*

'There's No Home For You Here' – *So it helps to have a mirror in the room*

SCHOOL/SCHOOLS

'Sister, Do You Know My Name?' – *Well we're back in school again…* and *I didn't see you at summer school*

'We're Going To Be Friends' – *Safely walk to school without a sound*

'The Air Near My Fingers' – *I never have to listen to the rings of school bells*

SISTER/BROTHER

'One More Cup of Coffee' (Dylan) – *Your sister sees the future like your mama and yourself*

'Screwdriver' – Think about your little sister… and *I love people like a brother now*

'Sister, Do You Know My Name?' – *Sister do you know my name?*

'Well It's True That We Love One Another' – *I love Jack White like a little brother*

TELEPHONE/PHONE

'A Boy's Best Friend' – *Empty rooms and a telephone that I will never use, never fear*

'Hello Operator' – *Nobody to answer the phone…* and *My coffin doesn't have a phone*

'Hypnotize' – *I want to hypnotize you baby on the telephone*

'I Can Learn' – *Drive you home, then wait by the phone*

'I'm Bound To Pack It Up' – *You're sitting silent by the phone*

'I Want To Be The Boy That Warms Your Mother's Heart' – *Because somebody ripped out my page in your telephone book*

'Little Bird' – *Put her in a cage and disconnect the phone*

'Screwdriver' – *I call him on the telephone*

'Well It's True That We Love One Another' – *I got your phone number written in the back of my bible*

TINY

'Dead Leaves And The Dirty Ground' – *And every little breath that is in your lungs is a tiny little gift to me*

'Truth Doesn't Make A Noise' – *The motion of her tiny hands*

TREE

'I Can Learn' – *I wish we were stuck up a tree*

'I'm Finding It Harder To Be A Gentleman' – *Every single girl needs help climbing up a tree*

'Girl, You Have No Faith In Medicine' – *Well strip the bark right off a tree*

TROUBLES/PROBLEMS

'Apple Blossom' – *All the ones you tell your troubles to / they don't really care for you…* and *You've been looking all around for years for someone to tell your troubles to..* and *Put your troubles in a little pile and I will sort them out for you*

'Little Acorns' – *Take all your problems and rip 'em apart…* and *The problems at hand are lighter than at heart…* and *Your problems hide in your curls*

Discography

WHITE STRIPES ALBUMS

The White Stripes (US June 1999, Sympathy For The Record Industry / UK December 2001, XL) – The blues-and-primitive-beat-driven debut that will always be a favorite for many, including The White Stripes themselves. (The original vinyl album has only 14 tracks, and was bolstered for the CD version by the addition of the US single tracks 'Sugar Never Tasted So Good' and 'The Big Three Killed My Baby,' as well as Dylan's 'One More Cup Of Coffee.')

De Stijl (US June 2000, Sympathy For The Record Industry / UK December 2001, XL) – A more luscious and teensy-bit layered White Stripes. (In the UK, both *De Stijl* and *The White Stripes* were released after the success of the third album, *White Blood Cells*.)

White Blood Cells (US July 2001, Sympathy For The Record Industry / UK July 2001, XL) – Recorded in three days, White Blood Cells heralded the return of primitive rock to the top of the charts in 2001 and introduced The White Stripes to the world. This blues-less, all-original wonder is The White Stripes' coming-of-age recording.

Elephant (US March 2003, V2-Third Man / UK March 2003, XL) – By combining the attitude of garage with the spirit of punk and the riffs of the heaviest metal, on *Elephant* The White Stripes freshen up metal for the modern age and help it transcend its reputation as dumb and sexist. (Available either as a double vinyl album – one disc red, the other white – or plain old 14-track CD.)

WHITE STRIPES SINGLES & EPs

'Let's Shake Hands'/'Look Me Over Closely' (Italy, April 1998; re-released in 2000)

'Lafayette Blues'/'Sugar Never Tasted So Good' (Italy, November 1998; re-released in 2001) – a highly collectable item. A very small number of the original edition were pressed on swirly red-and-white vinyl and issued in a hand-painted sleeve: if you have one of those it could be worth $600. Another 40 contained a French franc note.

'Xmas Surprise Package Vol 2' (Flying Bomb, November 1998) – a three-band compilation that includes the Stripes' 'Candy Cane Children.'

'The Big Three Killed My Baby'/'Red Bowling Ball Ruth' (Sympathy For The Record Industry, April 1999)

'Handsprings' (free with *Multiball* fanzine, March 2000) – the b-side was a track by The Dirtbombs.

'Hello Operator'/'Jolene' (Sympathy For The Record Industry, May 2000)

'Lord Send Me An Angel'/'You're Pretty Good Looking (Trendy American Remix)' (Sympathy For The Record Industry, October 2000; re-released in 2001)

'Party Of Special Things To Do'/'China Pig'/'Ashtray Heart' (Sub Pop, December 2000) – limited edition Captain Beefheart tribute.

'Dead Leaves And The Dirty Ground'/'Fell In Love With A Girl'/'Hotel Yorba' (Sympathy For The Record Industry, May 2001)

'It Takes Two Baby' (Sympathy For The Record Industry, May 2001) – various artists EP, includes 'Fell In Love With A Girl.'

'White Blood Cells Bonus Tracks EP' (V2 promo, June 2001) – includes 'Jolene,' 'Handsprings,' and live versions of 'Hotel Yorba' and 'Love Sick.'

'Hotel Yorba'/'Rated X' (XL/V2, November 2001)

'Fell In Love With A Girl'/'I Just Don't Know What To Do With Myself' (XL, February 2002) – also issued as a double CD with six tracks plus the Lego video.

'Dead Leaves And The Dirty Ground'/'Suzy Lee (Live)'/'Stop Breaking Down (Live)' (XL, UK, August 2002) – also issued as a DVD, including video.

'Red Death At 6:14' (XL/Mojo, August 2002) – one-track, red vinyl single available by mail to readers of UK magazine *Mojo*.

Originally on the various artists' compilation *Sympathetic Sounds Of Detroit*.

'Merry Christmas From The White Stripes' (V2/XL, December 2002) – limited edition EP, includes 'Candy Cane Children,' 'Reading Of The Story Of The Magi,' and 'Singing Of Silent Night.'

'Seven Nation Army'/'Good To Me' (V2/XL, March/ April 2003) – CD version includes the track 'Black Jack Davey,' a traditional folk song once covered by Dylan.

'I Just Don't Know What To Do With Myself'/'Who's To Say' (XL, September 2003) – alternative versions (on CD and/or DVD) add one or more of 'Lafayette Blues (Live),' 'Black Math (Live),' and 'I'm Finding It Harder To Be A Gentleman (Live).'

'The Hardest Button To Button'/'St Ides Of March' (V2/XL, October/ November 2003) – the b-side is a cover of a Soledad Brothers song.

OTHER RECOMMENDED RECORDINGS:
Various Artists: Sympathetic Sounds Of Detroit (Sympathy For The Record Industry, 2001) This Jack White-produced 19-song collection is the perfect intro to the world of beat-up, broken-down, super-rockin' new Detroit rock: the Paybacks' glammed-up 'Black Girl,' The Dirtbombs' big-beat 'I'm Through With White Girls,' the Soledad Brothers' electric-charged 'Shaky Puddin','' and The Detroit Cobras' cover of Little Richard's 'Shout Bama Lama.' It's the sound of Detroit today.

Various Artists: Anthology Of American Folk Music (Smithsonian Folkways Recordings, 1997) Originally released on six LPs in 1952 this served as a bible for the Sixties folk revivalists and helped re-launch the careers of the oldest living bluesmen. Compiled by archivist/ alchemist Harry Smith, it includes White Stripes' favorites like The Masked Marvel (Charley Patton) recording 'Mississippi Boweavil Blues' and Blind Willie Johnson's 'John The Revelator,' among other standards of the US folk tradition, from 'John Hardy' by the Carter Family to 'Spike Driver Blues' by Mississippi John Hurt.

Blind Willie McTell: 1927-1933 The Early Years (Yazoo, 1989) and *Blind Willie McTell: 1940* (Document, 1990) These two discs have the Georgia 12-string player's selections that will be of most interest to White Stripes fans. *The Early Years* includes 'Southern Can Is Mine' and 'Talkin' To Myself (Lord Send Me An Angel)' along with his 'greatest hit,' 'Statesboro Blues.' The 1940 record includes the 'Dying Crapshooter's Blues,' 'Boll Weevil' and the 'Monologue On Accidents' from the interview with John Lomax (as heard on *De Stijl*).

Son House: Martin Scorsese Presents The Blues (Columbia/Legacy, 2003) The title might not sound that credible, but this 2003 collection released in connection with the Scorsese-produced PBS television series has the essential Son House recordings, in chronological order, from the earliest versions like 'My Black Mama, Pt 1' and 'Preachin'

Blues, Pt 1' to his final 1965 recordings of 'Death Letter' and 'Grinnin' In Your Face.' Great introduction to one of Jack White's all-time blues heroes.

Blind Willie Johnson: Praise God I'm Satisfied (Yazoo, 1989) Jack's favorite slide guitarist, Johnson recorded this uplifting set of spiritual songs throughout the 1920s: it's all here: 'Jesus Make Up My Dying Bed,' 'Nobody's Fault But Mine,' 'Jesus Is Coming Soon,' and 'Motherless Children Have A Hard Time.'

The Yardbirds: Having A Rave-Up With The Yardbirds (Epic, 1965) Among British blues-rock albums, this Giorgio Gomelsky production is the pick for its wealth of hits and its influence on garage rock and hard rock lead guitar. It stands alongside the best work of The Rolling Stones and The Beatles and includes such powerful bluesy classics as 'Train Kept A Rollin',' 'Smokestack Lightnin',' and the jangly 'Heart Full Of Soul.'

Iggy & The Stooges: The Stooges (Elektra, 1969), *Fun House* (Elektra, 1970) The Stooges' second album, *Fun House*, is the one Jack and Meg swear by and it's no wonder: a lo-tech wonder, it captures the unwieldy mayhem of a Stooges gig and is driven by the beat of Scott Ashton's drums. The band and most critics disavow their John Cale-produced debut, yet it's a rock'n'roll classic, featuring 'No Fun' and 'I Wanna Be Your Dog.'

MC5: The Big Bang! Best Of The MC5 (Rhino, 2000) This telescoped version of the mighty fine Motor City Five's output from 1967-1971 is a great place to start for the uninitiated. White Stripes fans may be bowled over at just how much of the five-man band's spirit the two-piece capture. Beginning with an early single version of garage classic 'I Can Only Give You Everything,' through their third and final back-to-rock'n'roll-basics studio album *High Time*, the MC5 consistently kick out the jams.

Bob Dylan: Blood On The Tracks (Columbia, 1975); **Desire** (Columbia, 1976) Both albums have lore associated with the break-up of Dylan's marriage to Sara. The more personal *Blood On The Tracks* is Meg's all-time favorite; *Desire*, a mixture of fantasy and fable, is the source of the covers 'One More Cup Of Coffee' and 'Isis.'

The Gun Club: Fire Of Love (Slash/Rhino, 1981) The punk blues of LA's Gun Club was an early marriage of country blues and back-to-basics fury of primitive rock and Seventies punk. Singer/writer Jeffrey Lee Pierce rearranged Robert Johnson's 'Preaching The Blues' and Tommy Johnson's 'Cool Drink Of Water' for the post-Stones/Yardbirds and pre-Stripes generation.

Beck: Odelay (DGC, 1996); **Mutations** (DGC, 1998) This mega-selling album and its understated follow-up – the period that yielded sound collages from 'Devil's Haircut' to 'Bottle Of Blues' – might seem odd choices here. Yet Beck had a hand in modernizing country blues (albeit with an approach very different than the Stripes'), and he was responsible for the smartest and hippest sounds in rock at the time.

Soledad Brothers: Live (Dim Mak, 2003) Jack White produced this seven-song live set from the Gold Dollar by Toledo's Soledad Brothers: Johnny Walker on guitar, Ben Swank on drums, and new addition Oliver Henry on sax and guitar. They fuse the energy of early British blues-rock pioneers and a hard-driving electric blues sound to create their own unique Detroit rock blend, best showcased on 'Goin' Back To Memphis' (often covered by the Stripes) and the Stonesy 'Teenage Heart Attack.'

The Von Bondies: Raw And Rare (Dim Mak/In The Act, 2003) Foreboding Motor City rock rides again in the hands of the Jason Stollsteimer-led garage rockin' four-piece. Mostly recorded over two BBC sessions: Nov 2001, and May 2002. The Von Bondies are best heard in their element – live and unadulterated.

Index

A

Adams, Ryan 66
'Air Near My Fingers, The' 143
Airline guitar 18, 85
alternative music 73
'Aluminum' 105
Amboy Dukes 55
Animals, The 62
Anthology Of American Folk Music compilation 75, 89, 92-93
'Apple Blossom' 82, 138
'Ashtray Heart' 84

B

'Baby Blue' 113
Baby Killers, The 110
'Ball And Biscuit' 61, 62, 91, 129, 137
'Ballad Of Hollis Brown, The' 63

Bangs, Lester 11
Bantam Rooster 21, 24, 56, 108, 161
BBC radio sessions 30, 79, 113, 143
Beatles, The 55, 67
Beck 74-75, 153
Beck, Jeff 120
Benson, Brendan 138, 161
'Big Three Killed My Baby, The' 30, 89
'Black Jack Davey' 64
'Black Math' 129, 152
Black Rebel Motorcycle Club 66-67
Blanche 138
blues 16, 17, 28, 29, 60, 66, 70, 72, 74-75, 77-78, 91, 100, 101, 123, 158, 159
Blues Incorporated 60-61

'Bo(ll) Weevil (Song/Holler/Blues)' 65, 113, 149-150
'Boy's Best Friend, A' 83
Brand, Bruce 128
British blues-rock 60-62
Buick, Dave 24-26, 121, 152, 161

C

'Cannon' 30
Captain Beefheart 84
car industry 7, 9, 30, 89
Case, Wendy 108
Cash, Johnny 156
Catalyst 15
Childish, Billy 56
'China Pig' 84
Citizen Kane movie 103-104
Clinton, George 10
Coffee & Cigarettes movie 153

Cold Mountain movie 121-122, 134
Collins, Mick 108
colors, importance of 86-89
Coppola, Sofia 154
Count Five 55
Cramps, The 23, 31, 56
Cream 17, 61, 141
Creem magazine 11

D
Dale, Dick 55
Davis, Reverend Gary 64
De Stijl album 72, 77-86, 94, 97, 118, 119
De Stijl art movement 70-71, 72
'Dead Leaves And The Dirty Ground' 105, 107, 117
'Death Letter' 72, 79, 80, 113, 148
Demolition Doll Rods 21, 57
Detroit 6-11, 14-15, 17, 20-21, 30, 32, 55, 56, 57, 59, 60, 62, 95, 108-111, 118-119, 152, 160-161
Detroit Cobras, The 27, 61, 108, 110, 161
'Devil's Haircut' 157
Dexter Romweber Trio, The 52-53
Diamond, Jim 28, 72
Dickinson, Jim 102
Dirtbombs, The 108
'Don't Blame Me' 54
Doo Rag 29, 75, 77
Dylan, Bob 17, 28, 62-67, 158

E
Easley-McCain studio 101
Electric Prunes, The 56
Electric Six 154
Elephant album 127-145, 151
Eminem 118
Estrus Records 26
'Expecting' 105, 106

F
Faulkner, Jason 138
'Fell In Love With A Girl' 105, 117, 149
Fischer, Dion 152, 161
'Fist City' 136
Flat Duo Jets, 18, 52-53, 54, 102
Foster, Stephen 133
'From A Buick Six' 17
Fun House album 57
Funkadelic 10

G
garage rock 54-57
Ghetto Recorders studio 28, 72
Gillis, John 14
'Girl You Have No Faith In Medicine' 143
Girlie Action publicists 112
Glastonbury show 149
Go, The 25
'Goin' Back To Memphis' 79
Golightly, Holly 56, 128, 130
Gondry, Michel 117, 152
Goober & The Peas 18-19, 134
'Good To Me' 138
Gories, The 18, 21, 56, 108
Grammy nominations 144
Greenhornes, The 115, 120, 130
'Grinnin' In Your Face' 79, 80, 149, 151, 159
'Groom Still Waiting At The Altar' 17
'Groove Holmes' 17
guitar
slide/steel 30, 82, 83, 134
tunings 137
Gun Club, The 18, 29, 56, 110

H
'Hardest Button To Button, The' 67, 129, 142, 152
Harris, Emmylou 22
'Heart Full Of Soul' 120
'Hello Operator' 72, 81, 113
Hendrix, Jimi 62, 86-87, 137
Henry, Oliver 115
Hentchmen, The 21, 24, 56, 108, 128
Hooker, John Lee 8, 17, 62
'Hotel Yorba' 106, 134
House, Son 31, 64, 76, 79-80, 145, 159
Houston, David 56
Howlin' Wolf 17
'Hypnotize' 142-143

I
'I Ain't Done Wrong' 120
'I Can Only Give You Everything' 157
'I Fought Piranhas' 31
'I Just Don't Know What To Do With Myself' 143, 154
'I Think I Smell A Rat' 15, 105

Iggy Pop 10, 19, 22, 57-58, 86
Iggy & The Stooges 10, 57-58, 154, 160
'I'm Bound To Pack It Up' 82-83, 137
'I'm Finding It Harder To Be A Gentleman' 82, 106-107, 138
'In The Cold Cold Night' 143
indie rock 73
'Isis' 63
'It Can't Be Love Because There Is No True Love' 103
Italy Records 24, 25
'It's True That We Love One Another' 130

J
'Jack The Ripper' 31
'Jimmy The Exploder' 28, 134
'John The Revelator' 30-31, 75, 76, 80, 91, 149
'Johnny's Death Letter' 26
Johnson, Blind Willie 30, 64, 75
Johnson, Robert 28, 29, 64
'Jolene' 81, 134
Jones, Brian 55
'Jumble Jumble' 83, 137

K
Kaye, Lenny 56
Kingsmen, The 55
Kinks, The 78

L
'Lafayette Blues' 26
Lawrence, Jack 120
Leadbelly 75, 105, 150
Led Zeppelin 16, 61-62, 137
'Let's Build A Home' 78-79, 83
'Let's Shake Hands' 26, 79, 113, 137
'Little Acorns' 82, 143
'Little Bird' 81-82
'Little People' 31, 137
'Little Room' 106
Lollapalooza show 149
Long Gone John 27-28, 115-116
'Look Me Over Closely' 26
'Looking At You' 18
'Lord Send Me An Angel' 95
'Loser' 75
'Louie Louie' 55
'Louisiana Woman

Mississippi Man' 136
'Lovesick' 63
Lynn, Loretta 22, 83, 135-136, 153-154

M

Mamas & The Papas, The 130
'Man' 157
'Masters Of War' 17
McDonald, Steven 66
McDowell, Mississippi Fred 77
MC5, The 10, 18, 26, 57, 58-60
McTell, Blind Willie 31, 64, 66, 94-96, 130, 150
Memphis 101-102
Metallica shows 149
Milkshakes, The 56
Miller, Dan 19, 134, 138
minstrelsy 65
Mondrian, Piet 70-71
Montone, Ian 112
Motown 8-9, 110-111
MTV Awards 118, 152
Muddy Waters 60, 75
Muldoon, Brian 18

N

'96 Tears' 54
Nirvana 74, 75
'Now Mary' 103
Nuggets compilations 56
numbers, importance of 89-92

O

'One More Cup Of Coffee' 28, 31, 63, 83
Ossy, Paul Henry 83
Ozzfest show 149

P

Page, Jimmy 61
Parliament 10
'Party Of Special Things To Do' 84
Patton, Charlie 64, 160
Pavement 26
Paybacks, The 108, 161
Peel sessions *see* BBC radio sessions
Peppermint Triple Tremelo cabinet 85
'Peter Gunn' 31
Phillips, Sam 101
'Pick A Bale Of Cotton' 157
Plant, Robert 61-62

Porter, Cole 139-140
Public Nuisance 55-56
punk 57, 58, 72
Pussy Galore 56, 76

Q

? & The Mysterians 54

R

Rainey, Ma 81, 150
'Rated X' 83, 134, 136
'Ready Teddy' 157
Redd Kross 66
religion 65, 86
Rocket-455 21, 56
'Rockhouse' 54
Rodgers, Jimmy 136-137
Rolling Stones, The 29, 61, 121
Romweber, Dexter 52
Rube Waddell 75

S

'St Ides Of March' 137
'St James Infirmary Blues' 28, 31-32, 148
'Same Boy You've Always Known' 137
Saturday Night Live 121
Screaming Lord Sutch 31
'Screwdriver' 23-24, 113
Seeds, The 56
Seger, Bob 55, 141
'Seven Nation Army' 89, 91, 93, 129, 131, 141-142, 144, 151, 152
Shaw, Steve 27
Silvertone amplifier 18
Sinclair, John 26, 59
'Sister Do You Know My Name' 83
'Sittin' On Top Of The World' 17, 61, 122
Sleater-Kinney 27
'Slicker Drips' 31
'Small Faces' song 55
Smith, Harry 75, 92, 93
Soledad Brothers, 25, 26, 55, 108, 115, 137, 153, 157
Sonic Youth 74
Spand, Charlie 8
Spencer, Jon 29, 56, 76
Stollsteimer, Jason 24, 109-110, 120, 161
'Stop Breaking Down' 28-29

Strokes, The 118
Suchyta, Dominic 16, 18
'Sugar And Spice' 26
'Sugar Never Tasted So Good' 26
Sun Ra 60
'Suzy Lee' 31
Swank, Ben 25, 77
Sympathetic Sounds Of Detroit compilation 57, 108
Sympathy for The Record Industry label 27, 108, 112-113, 115-116
Syzmanski, John 81

T

T In The Park show 149
'Take A Whiff On Me' 105
Tampa Red 64
'That's Where It's At' 105
Thee Headcoats/Headcoatees 56, 75
'There's No Home For You Here' 129, 143-144
Third Man studio/label 71, 104, 115
Third Man, The movie 90, 104, 156
13th Floor Elevators 55
ToeRag studio 128
'Train Kept A Rollin', The' 120
Troggs, The 55
'Truth Doesn't Make A Noise' 83
Tucker, Mo 22, 83
Two Part Resin 18
Two Star Tabernacle 25, 103, 122, 134

U

'Unfortunate Rake, The' 31
'Union Forever, The' 103, 105

V

Van Doesburg, Theo 70
Vaughan, Stevie Ray 16
Ventures, The 55
Von Bondies, The 24, 108, 109-110, 113, 116, 119-120, 161
V2 Records label 115

W

Walker, Johnny 25, 31, 77, 137
Watson, Liam 128
'Wayfaring Stranger' 122
'We're Going To Be Friends' 83, 105, 106

Weiss, Janet 27
'When I Hear My Name' 30, 137
Whirlwind Heat 115
White Blood Cells album 85, 100-108, 112, 116, 119, 123, 134
White Blood Cells DVD 127
White Panther Party 59
White Stripes, The album 28-32, 118
'Who's To Say' 138

'Why Can't You Be Nicer To Me' 78, 84
Williams, André 110
Williamson, Sonny Boy 62
Witness show 149
'Words Of Love' 157

Y

Yardbirds, The 61, 120

Yeah Yeah Yeahs, The 157
'Your Southern Can Is Mine' 72, 94-95, 137
'You're Pretty Good Looking' 78, 82
'You've Got Her In Your Pocket' 129, 143

Acknowledgements

Source material for quotes –
Author interviews with: Dave Buick, Holly Golightly, Oliver Henry, Dexter Romweber, Jason Stollsteimer, Dominic Suchyta, Ben Swank, Johnny Walker, and Janet Weiss.

And from the following sources: *The Necessity For Ruins, And Other Topics,* J.B. Jackson, University Of Massachusetts Press, 1980; *American Ruins,* Camilio Jose Vergara, The Monacelli Press, 1999; 'Under The Red Sky' by Bob Dylan, Special Rider Music; 'White Stripes Love Hot Dogs,' by Amber Dawn Everson, *Hot Dog #1,* Spring 2001; 'Pure & Simple,' by Michael Odell, *Q,* June 2003; 'Sister? Lover? An Interview With The White Stripes' by Jennifer Maerz, *spin.com,* June 5th 2001; 'White Heat' by Darrin Fox, *Guitar Player,* June 2003; 'The White Stripes: Jack White Talking' by Kurt Hernon, *bangsheet.com;* 'Your Furniture Is Not Dead," by Tobias de la Manzana, *The Believer,* May 2003; 'King & Queen Of Rock!' by Andrew Perry, *Blender,* May 2003; 'A Label All His Own – Long Gone John, Indie Rock's Anti-Mogul' by David Segal, *Washington Post,* May 28th 2003; A Definitive Oral History: Revealing the White Stripes by Brian McCollum, Detroit Free Press, April 13th 2003; 'The White Stripes' by Lennart Persson, *Sonic* magazine (translated by Cassie & Johan Berglund, *tripletremelo.com*); 'Basic Instinct,' by Andrew Male, *Mojo,* September 2002; 'The White Stripes' by Jim Jarmusch, *Interview,* May 2003; John Lennon quote from *Lennon Remembers,* Jann S. Wenner, Straight Arrow Books, 1971; 'White Stripes Blow Up With Red, White & Blues,' by Brian Wallace, *mtv.com,* July 18th 2001; 'White Stripes Stick To Primary Colors, Ideas, Sounds,' by Chris Nelson, *vh1.com,* March 23rd 2000; Willamette Week Online (wweek.com); bbc.co.uk; two quotes in Orson Welles section from: *This is Orson Welles Orson Welles & Peter Bogdanovich* Harper-Collins, 1992; 'White On Time,' by Trevor Kelley, *Devil In The Woods,* Issue 5.2; 'Black And White And Red All Over,' by Jay Ruttenberg, *Time Out New York,* March 27th-April 3rd 2003; Robert Plant quote from 'Been A Long Time' by Barney Hoskyns, *Mojo,* June 2003; 'All Back To My Place; Meg White,' *Mojo,* March 2003; 'The Motor City Two,' by Ian Winwood, *Kerrang!,* Dec 15th 2001; 'Rock'n'Rules' by Hugo Lindgren, *New York Times Magazine,* March 9th 2003; 'White Stripes Invade New York' by Austin Scaggs, *Rolling Stone;* 'We Thought It Was Going To Destroy Us' by James Oldham, *NME,* March 1st 2003; 'Leaving Trunk,' *Mojo,* March 2003; 'Rated-X-traordinary' by Greg Crawford, *Detroit Free Press,* June 27th 2003; 'Jack White Produces Country Star...', by Jon Wiederhorn with Meridith Gottlieb, August 26th 2003, *mtv.com;* 'An Indie To The Core – Long Gone John's Obsession...' by Dean Kuipers, *Los Angeles Times,* Jan 19th 2003; 'Made In Detroit,' by Jonathan Perry, *Boston Globe,* April 11th 2003; 91X, Atlanta, on-air interview, June 2003; 'Jack's Back,' by John Mulvey, *NME,* September 27th 2003; 'Iggy Pop On Life, Lust And Rock'n'Roll' by Jack White with Keith Cameron, *Mojo,* October 2003; 'Detroit Sweats While It Waits For Electricity' by Jodi Wilgoren & Danny Hakim, *New York Times,* August 16th 2003; 'TheCoppola Smart Mob' by Lynn Hirschberg, *New York Times Magazine,* August 31st 2003; 'All Stars And Stripes!', *nme.com,* September 7th 2003; 'Rock Duo Postpones Tour Dates' Reuters, July 15th 2003; *Pollstar,* April 15th 2002; 'White Stripes Sticking To The Basics,' cnn.com, August 14th 2003; 'The White Stripes: Candy Coloured Blues' DVD, Chrome Dreams, 2003; *Son House & Bukka White; Masters Of The Country Blues,* DVD, Yazoo, 2000; 'Sweetheart Of The Blues' by Lennat Mak, *mtvasia.com,* Nov 2003; 'White Riot' by Simon Goddard, *Record Collector,* Nov 2003; Ben Schmitt, *Detroit Free Press,* Dec 16-17th 2003.

The following websites, official and otherwise, were also useful:
www.whitestripes.com
www.whitestripes.net
www.tripletremelo.com
www.expecting.com

Other works consulted:
White Boy Singin' The Blues – The Black Roots Of White Rock, Michael Bane, Da Capo, 1992; *Red River Blues, The Blues Tradition In The Southeast,* Bruce Bastin, University of Illinois Press, 1995; *A Treasury of American Folklore – Stories, Ballads &*

Traditions Of The People, Ed B.A. Botkin, Crown Publishers, 1944; *Don't Let Me Be Misunderstood*, Eric Burdon with Marshall J. Craig, Thunder's Mouth Press, 2001; *Bluegrass Breakdown – The Making Of The Old Southern Sound*, Robert Cantwell, Da Capo Press, 1992; *Poetry Of The Blues*, Samuel Charters, Avon, 1963; *The Country Blues*, Samuel B. Charters, Da Capo, 1975; *Blues Legacies And Black Feminism: Gertrude 'Ma' Rainey, Bessie Smith, and Billie Holiday*, Angela Y. Davis, Pantheon Books, 1998; *I Am The Blues – The Willie Dixon Story*, Willie Dixon with Don Snowden, Da Capo, 1989; *The Book Of Prophecy*, Edward Edelson, Doubleday & Co, 1974; *Doo-Dah! Stephen Foster And The Rise Of American Popular Culture*, Ken Emerson, Da Capo, 1998; *Good Rockin' Tonight – Sun Records And The Birth Of Rock'n'Roll*. Colin Escott with Martin Hawkins, St Martin's Press, 1991; *Blues And The Poetic Spirit*, Paul Garon, City Lights, 1975/1996; *The Elements Of Alchemy*, Gilchrist, Cherry, Element Books, 1991; *Song & Dance Man III: The Art Of Bob Dylan*, Michael Gray, Cassell, 2000; *The Algiers Motel Incident*, John Hersey, John Hopkins University Press, 1968; *Blues People – Negro Music In White America*, LeRoi Jones, (Amiri Baraka), Quill, 1999; *Folk Songs Of North America*, Alan Lomax, Doubleday, 1960; *The Land Where Blues Began*, Alan Lomax, Pantheon Books, 1993; *Love & Theft: Blackface & Minstrelsy & The American Working Class*, Eric Lott, Oxford University Press, 1993; *Invisible Republic – Bob Dylan's Basement Tapes*, Greil Marcus, Henry Holt, 1997; *Krazy Kat – The Comic Art Of George Herriman*, Patrick McDonnell, Karen O'Connell, Karen, Georgia Riley De Havenon, Harry N. Abrams Inc. 1986; *Blues Fell This Morning – Meaning In The Blues*, Paul Oliver, PCambridge University Press, 1960; *Screening The Blues: Aspects Of The Blues Tradition*, Paul Oliver, Da Capo, 1968; *The Story Of The Blues*, Paul Oliver, Penguin Books, 1972; *Jimi Hendrix – Electric Gypsy*, Harry Shapiro & Caesar Glebbeck, St Martin's Griffin, 1995; *A Booklet Of Essays, Appreciations, & Annotations Pertaining To The Anthology Of American Folk Music*, ed Harry Smith, Smithsonian Folkways Recordings, Washington, DC, 1997.

Photographs used are from the following sources –
Redferns: front cover – Jim Sharpe; p1/40/42 (top) and Von Bondies p35 – Tabatha Fireman; p4/12/50/68/98/ 124 – Michael Ochs Archive; p33/45 (bottom) – Hayley Madden; p99 – Ebet Roberts; p39 (t)/45 (t) – Nicky J. Sims; p39 (b) – Bob King; p42 (bottom two) – Jon Super; p43 – Martin Philbey; Detroit pics, p5/13 – Photography Plus; **All other photos, including back cover – Doug Coombes.**

The author wishes to thank God, family, The White Stripes (Jack and Meg White), Soledad Brothers (Johnny Walker, Ben Swank and Oliver Henry), Jason Stollsteimer, Dave Buick, Holly Golightly, Dexter Romweber, Janet Weiss and Dominic Suchyta. Thank you to the writers and publications whose articles were quoted and whose work aided me in my research (see the sources list for specifics), particularly pieces by Andrew Male for *Mojo*, Darrin Fox for *Guitar Player*, Michael Odell for *Q* and Jim Jarmusch for *Interview*.

At Backbeat, I thank Tony Bacon and Nigel Osborne for their complete confidence in the project; Paul Cooper for design; plus Mark Brend and John Ryall in the UK and Kevin Becketti and Nina Lesowitz in the US. Thanks to my expert editor Paul Quinn for suggestions and patience.

The job could not have been completed without the help of many others, chiefly my true love Peter Case and my true friend Yvette Bozzini – their generosity knows no bounds, nor does my gratitude to both of them. Others who went into realms beyond the call of duty and to whom I am grateful: Lauren Catalena, Rachel Matthews, Erin O'Connor, Jaan Uhelzski, Velena Vego, Joan Wallace and Sue Whitehall. Thank you to: Jared Altschul, Steve Aoki, Nils Bernstein, Paul Bradshaw & Naomi Diamond at Mod Lang Records, Ian Brennen, Julie Butterfield, Joshua, Leah & Natalie Case, Doug Coombes, Sheila Dolan, Felice Ecker and Alison Zero at Girlie Action, Neil Feineman, Laurie & Bill Forbes, Tom Jurek, Howie Klein, Mary Kegg Fairweather, Sally Gehring, Dave Kaplan, Alan Korn, Dan Miller, Thessa Mooij, Brigid Pearson, Chuck Prophet & Stephanie Finch, Steve Martin, Ken Phillips, Phast Phreddie, Terry Reid, Bruce Solar, Sara St Martin Lynne, Katie Thigpen, Richie Unterberger, Maggie Vail, Troy Wallace, Andrea Wehenkel, Shell White & J.C. Hopkins, Willy Wilson, Chris Woodstra, and to you. Additional information, footnotes and fun facts surrounding *The White Stripes – Sweethearts of the blues* are posted at *www.denisesullivan.com*

Extract from:
The Ballad Of Jack And Meg

Guitar sound, drum beat
And a story to tell
Boy and girl in red and white and
Blues as well
God and love ride with them
While there're rumors to quell
Candy stripes and broken bricks
Does it ring any bells?

This is the story of Jack and Meg
For those who rock but
Oh, they're hard to peg
They never sought this kind of fame
They didn't know they'd come to save
Rock and all its ways...

"Though your sins they are like scarlet,
They shall be as white as snow"
Isaiah 1:18